THE E.Y. MULLINS LECTURES ON PREACHING WITH REFERENCE TO THE ARISTOTELIAN TRIAD

Don M. Aycock

University Press of America™

Copyright © 1980 by

University Press of America, Inc.
4710 Auth Place, S.E., Washington, D.C. 20023

ISBN: 0-8191-0981-9

Library of Congress Catalog Card Number: 79-6080

DEDICATION

Many persons and factors lay in the background of this book and must be acknowledged.
Some of these persons include Dr. George A.
Buttrick, Andrew McRae, Charles L. Holland, and
Dr. Edward L. Byrd. Dr. James W. Cox took me
on as one of his graduate students and helped
guide my studies at Southern Baptist Seminary
in Louisville, Kentucky. Dr. G. Earl Guinn
and Dr. Frank Tupper served on my advisory
committee. Dr. William P. Tuck joined this
committee at a pivotal stage and helped me more
than he will ever know. Dr. Ronald Deering
and the staff of the Boyce Library helped me
secure materials which were often difficult to
locate.

The people of West Side Baptist Church of
Louisville were most gracious and understanding
as their pastor "hibernated" to finish this
book. Finally, my beautiful wife Carla provided
both emotional and intellectual support for my
work. To her I dedicate this book.

iv

ACKNOWLEDGMENTS

I would like to thank the following persons and publishers for their permissions to use their materials:

Fortress Press, for use of passages from The Anguish of Preaching, Joseph Sittler, (C) 1966, used by permission of Fortress Press.
Harper and Row Publishers, for use of passages from The Making of the Sermon, Robert J. McCracken, (C) 1956, used by permission. The Word God Sent, Paul Scherer, (C) 1965, used by permission.
Princeton Theological Seminary, for use of passages from The Princeton Seminary Bulletin, (LXVIII, 2, 37), (C) 1975, "Theology Gives Meaning and Shape to Worship," by Donald Macleod, use by permission.
Princeton University Press, for use of passages from Worship And Theology In England: From Newman to Martineau, 1850-1900, "Worship and Theology In England," Vol. 4, Horton Davies, (C) 1962, used by permission of Princeton University Press.
Review and Expositor, XLIII, 3; XLIII, 4; XLIV, 1; used by permission of The Southern Baptist Theological Seminary.

The following persons have kindly allowed me to use their materials:

Dr. Theodore F. Adams
Dr. George A. Buttrick
Dr. John R. Claypool
Mr. Henry G. Davis, Jr.
Dr. H. H. Farmer
Dr. Roger Fredrikson
Dr. James I. McCord
Dr. John A. Mackay
Mr. William Miller
Dr. William Muehl

Mrs. Harold Cooke Phillips
Dr. Kelly Miller Smith

TABLE OF CONTENTS

INTRODUCTION

This book examines the E. Y. Mullins Lectures
on Preaching with reference to Aristotle's triadic
elements. Known classically as the "Aristotelian
triad," these three elements form the basis of
communication and include the speaker, speech,
and audience.[1] This triadic conception of the
communication process has been expanded recently
by communication theorists.[2] Since the purpose
of this book is not to debate that issue, the classical triadic elements will be utilized.

The purpose of this study is to answer the
question: "What has been said by the Mullins
lecturers about the speaker, the speech, and the
audience?" The work takes the form of an "analyt-
ical description" as noted by Carter V. Good and
Douglas E. Scates.[3]

Precedents for this kind of analysis include
B. B. Baxter's work, The Heart of the Yale Lectures,[4]
and Gaylord L. Lehman's, "The Themes of Preaching
in the Yale Lectures: 1900-1958."[5]

DEFINITION OF TERMS

The Aristotelian Triad is used pursuant to a
specifically Christian setting in general and a
local church context in particular.

Speaker
By "speaker" is meant the person who delivers
the message orally. The use of this term in this
study refers specifically to the preacher. Included
in the use of the word "speaker" are aspects of
his or her personality, qualifications, preparation, and attitudes.

Speech
"Speech" is the message which is given. In a
Christian context, it is the body of material presented, the sermon. Emphasis is given to defin-
ing the sermon's goals and methods, and to examin-
ing style, sources, delivery, and settings for the

1

sermon. Craftsmanship involved in writing the
sermon is studied also.

Audience
    "Audience" is that body of people who hear sermons
as orally delivered. It is the congregation, al-
though the term also refers to other groups of persons addressed by the Gospel.

BACKGROUND OF THE STUDY

    The E. Y. Mullins Lectures on Preaching came
to my attention during my first semester at Southern
Baptist Theological Seminary in Louisville, Kentucky.
In that year, 1974, Dr. John Claypool delivered a
series of lectures on the theme, "The Preaching
Event." Those lectures inspired me to investigate
other lectures in the Mullins series. What was
found was a large collection of lectures and sermons
from great preachers and scholars. Unfortunately,
many of these were placed in the library and for-
gotten. Others were never collected at all and are
now lost or are simply not available. Thus, I pro-
pose to gather together as many lectures as are
available and to trace three themes through them.

    This lecture series was made possible by a
grant willed to The Southern Baptist Theological
Seminary.[6] Mrs. Mullins added the sum of three
thousand dollars to the ten thousand dollars pre-
viously given by her husband and former president
of Southern Seminary, Dr. E. Y. Mullins. Dr.
Mullins, himself a noted preacher, had an abiding
interest in seeing the quality of preaching improve
among students at Southern Seminary and throughout
the Southern Baptist Convention.

    Dr. George A. Buttrick was invited to inaugur-
ate the lectures in 1937, but he replied that he
had to decline the invitation.[7] The first lectures
were actually given in the 1941-42 academic year
by William Lyon Phelps, professor emeritus of Yale
University. The lectures have continued annually,
with five exceptions. No lectures were given in
the academic years of 1943-44, 1949-50, 1950-51,

2

1958-59, and 1964-65.

Eight complete lecture series are available in unpublished manuscript form.[8] All or portions of sixteen series are available on reel-to-reel tape.[9] Portions of five of the series have been published in the <u>Review and Expositor</u>.[10] Six series have been published in book form.[11] Some persons invited to give the Mullins Lectures were given the option of presenting lectures or sermons. Six series were therefore not lectures at all but were sermons.[12] Six set of lectures and sermons are not available at all.[13] Thus, all or portions of twenty-six sets of lectures and sermons are available. A complete listing of all of the lectures, along with their themes, is included at the end of this chapter.

METHODOLOGY

All of the available lectures in the Mullins series are examined according to the stated purpose of this study, namely, to discover what has been said by the various lecturers about the speaker (preacher), the speech (sermon), and the audience (congregation). Upon examination, the sermons in the series have yielded little material relating to the themes of this study. For this reason the six sets of sermons are not utilized. This study is broad enough to deal with the lectures, but narrow enough to be specific and stay within the stated purposes of this study.

THE E. Y. MULLINS LECTURES
ON PREACHING

1. 1941-42, by William Lyon Phelps, Professor Emeritus of Yale University. Theme: "The Experience of Christian Religion in Literature." (Not available)

2. 1942-43, by George A. Buttrick, Pastor of the Madison Avenue Presbyterian Church, New York City. Lectures: I. "What Is The Gospel?" II. "Power-- and the Man." III. "The

3

Craftsmanship of Preaching. (A)" IV. "The
Craftsmanship of Preaching. (B)" V. "Preaching in This Present Age." (I and II are in
the Review and Expositor; III-V are not available. Dr. Buttrick loaned me his original
manuscript for this study.)

1943-44, not given.

3. 1944-45, by Halford E. Luccock, Professor at
    Yale Divinity School. Lectures: I. "What
    Literature Can Do For the Preacher." II.
    "A Hunger For Affirmations." III. "The Still
    Sad Music of Humanity." IV. "The Greatest
    Literature of All-- The Bible." V. "Litera-
    ture and the Sermon." (I and II and in the
    Review and Expositor; III-V are not available.)

4. 1945-46, by H. H. Farmer, Professor of Phil-
    osophy at Cambridge University. Theme: "The
    Source and Setting of the Sermon." Lectures:
    I. "Preaching and Worship." II. "The
    Preacher and Persons." III. "The Preacher
    and Culture." IV. "The Preacher and Books."
    V. "The Bible and Preaching." (I-III are
    in the Review and Expositor; IV-V are not
    available.)

5. 1946-47, by Charles L. Graham, Pastor of the
    Cresent Hill Baptist Church, Louisville,
    Kentucky. Sermons: I. "Despising the Shame."
    II. "God's Interpreters." III. "Good Man."
    IV. "Belshazzar's Feast." (Not available)

6. 1947-48, by John A. Mackay, President of Prince-
    ton Theological Seminary. Theme: "Our
    World and God's Gospel." Lectures: I. "The
    Life of Man in the Light of God." II. "God's
    Unveiled Secret." III. "The Cosmic Christ."
    IV. "The Gospel of God for the Nations."
    V. "Christian Action on the Frontiers of
    Strife." (Mimeographed)

7. 1948-49, by Elmer G. Homrighausen, Thomas
    Synnott Professor of Christian Education at

Princeton Theological Seminary. Theme:
"The Primary Task of the Church." Lectures:
I. "Why Engage In Evangelism?" II. "What
Is Evangelism?" III. "How Evangelize To-
day?" (Not available)

1949-50, not given.

1950-51, not given.

8. 1951-52, T. W. Manson, Professor at the Uni-
versity of Manchester, England. Theme:
"Some Aspects of the Public Ministry of
Jesus." (Book: <u>The Servant-Messiah</u>)

9. 1952-53, by Harold Cooke Phillips, Pastor
of the First Baptist Church of Cleveland,
Ohio. Lectures: I. "The Preacher and
the Gospel." II. "The Gospel in Hosea."
III. "The Preacher and the Church." IV.
"The Preacher and His Age." (Not available.)

10. 1953-54, by David A. MacLennan, Professor at
Yale Divinity School. Theme: "Pastoral
Preaching." Lectures: I. "Perspectives."
II. "Objectives." III. "Resources." IV.
"Methods." V. "The Pastor Preaching."
(Book: <u>Pastoral Preaching</u>)

11. 1954-55, by Robert J. McCracken, Minister of
the Riverside Church, New York City. Theme:
"The Making of the Sermon." Lectures: I.
"The Long-range Preparation of the Sermon."
II. "The Varied Character of the Sermon."
III. "Preaching As an Art." IV. "The Con-
struction of the Sermon." (Book: <u>The Mak-
ing of the Sermon</u>)

12. 1955-56, by Theodore F. Adams, Pastor of the
First Baptist Church, Richmond, Virginia.
Theme: "A Preacher Looks at His Preaching."
Lectures: I. "The Preacher Looks At
Himself and His People." II. "The Faith
of a Preacher." III. "Planning, Preparing,
and Preaching." IV. "Preaching With

Power and Purpose." (Mimeographed)

13. 1956-57, by Paul Scherer, Professor of
     Homiletics at Union Theological Seminary,
     New York City. Theme: "The Word in Search
     of Words." Lectures: I. "A Great Gulf
     Fixed." II. "The Nature of Revelation."
     III. "The Credibility and Relevance of the
     Gospel." IV. "Preaching as a Radical
     Transaction." (Mimeographed and book, The
     Word God Sent)

14. 1957-58, by Clarence W. Cranford, Pastor of
     the Calvary Baptist Church, Washington,
     D. C. Theme: "The Minister and His Task."
     Lectures: I. "The Pulpit Ministry." II.
     "The Minister and His Bible." III. "Don't
     Forgets for the Minister." IV. "The Min-
     ister and His World." (Not available)

     1958-59, not given.

15. 1959-60, by G. Earl Guinn, President, Louisi-
     ana College. Lectures: I. "Reformation
     Preaching." II. "That the Ministry Might
     Not Be Ashamed." (I not available, II mimeo-
     graphed)

16. 1960-61, by Horton Davies, Professor of
     Religion at Princeton University. Theme:
     "The Power of the Victorian Pulpit."
     (Chapter X of Worship and Theology in Eng-
     land, Vol. 4.

17. 1961-62, by H. Grady Davis, Professor of
     Homiletics at Chicago Lutheran Seminary.
     Theme: "Reappraisals of Preaching. "
     Lectures: I. "The Personal Word." II.
     "The Contemporary Word." III. "The Indi-
     vidual and Community." IV. "The Moment of
     Recognition." (Mimeographed)

18. 1962-63, by Samuel H. Miller, Dean, Harvard

Divinity School. Theme: "The Minister's
Workmanship." Lectures: I. "The Word of
God - And Words." II. "The Vision of
Reality - And Art." III. "The Care of
Souls - And Faith." IV. "The Insight of
Saints - And Morals." (Mimeographed)

19. 1963-64, by Harold Cooke Phillips, Pastor
Emeritus of the First Baptist Church of
Cleveland, Ohio. Lectures: I. "The
Eternal Word." II. "The Relevant Word."
III. "The Word of God." IV. "Communi-
cating the Word of God." (Mimeographed)

   1964-65, not given.

20. 1965-66, by Joseph Sittler, Professor of The-
ology, Lutheran School of Theology of Chicago.
Lectures: I. "The Role of the Seminary
in the Formation of the Preacher." II. "The
Problems of New Testament Interpretation
and the Task of the Preacher." III. "The
Anguish of Christology." IV. "Faith and
Form." (Book: The Anguish of Preaching)

21. 1966-67, by Elam Davis, Pastor of the Fourth
Avenue Presbyterian Church, Chicago. Sermons: I. "The God Who Creates From Nothing." II. "On Treating People as Persons." III. "The Church and the Social
Dilemma." IV. "God and Life." (Tape
recordings)

22. 1967-68, by J. P. Allen, Pastor of the Broadway Baptist Church, Ft. Worth, Texas. Sermons: I. "What Kind of Gospel?" II. "The
Next to Last Straw." III. "Life's Indefinable Categories." IV. "Open Other Channels."
(Tape recordings)

23. 1968-69, by Jack Finegan, Professor of New
Testament and Archaeology, Pacific School
of Religion. Sermons: I. "God, Jesus,
and Life." II. "With Whom There is No

7

Variableness." III. "Measuring Jeru-
salem." (Tape recordings)

24. 1969-70, by Donald Macleod, Professor of Homi-
letics, Princeton Theological Seminary.
Lectures: I. "Crisis in Preaching." II.
"The Identity of the Preacher." III. "The
Preacher at Worship." IV. "What Are You
Doing in Church?" (Tape recordings)

25. 1970-71, by Kelley Miller Smith, Pastor of
the Capitol Hill First Baptist Church,
Nashville, Tennessee. Theme: "Preaching
and Social Crises." Lectures: I. "What
Social Crises?" II. "Through a Glass
Blackly." III. "The Relevance of Structure." (Tape recordings)

26. 1971-72, by Edmund Steimle, Brown Professor
of Homiletics at Union Theological Seminary,
New York City. Sermons: I. "Lover's
Quarrel." II. "Children and Angels." III.
"The Waiting Game." (Tape recordings)

27. 1972-73, by D. E. King, Pastor of the Monu-
mental Baptist Church, Chicago, Illinois.
Sermon theme: "Creative Preaching." (Not
available)

28. 1973-74, by John R. Claypool, Pastor of the
Broadway Baptist Church, Ft. Worth, Texas.
Theme: "The Preaching Event." Lectures:
I. "Preaching and the Preacher." II.
"The Authority of the Preacher." III.
"Listening and Preaching." IV. "From
Preaching to Liturgies." (Tape recordings)

29. 1974-75, by William Muehl, Professor of
Homiletics, Yale Divinity School. Lectures:
I. "A Sense of Loss." II. "The Height
of Creativity." III. "The Depth of Judg-
ment." IV. "The Breadth of Compassion."
(Tape recordings)

30. 1975-76, by Roger Fredrikson, Pastor of the First Baptist Church, Wichita, Kansas. Theme: "Renewal in the Church." Lectures: I. "Renewal." II. "Following Him: What Will He Make of Us?" III. "Look Who's Coming to the Party." (Tape recordings)

31. 1976-77, by James I. McCord, President, Princeton Theological Seminary. Theme: "Theological Education and the Preacher." Lectures: I. "The Anthropolotical Question." II. "The Christological Answer." III. "Liberation Theology."

32. 1977-78, by Clyde Fant, Pastor of the First Baptist Church, Richardson, Texas. Theme: "The Authentic Voice In Preaching." (Tape recordings)

33. 1978-79, Gardner C. Taylor, Pastor of the Concord Baptist Church of Christ, Brooklyn, New York. Lectures: I. "The Preacher and the Preacher's Themes." II. "A Model For Preaching." III. "The Soul of the Preacher." IV. "Can These Bones Live Again?" (Tape recordings)

FOOTNOTES

[1]The Rhetoric of Aristotle, trans. by Lane
Cooper, (New York: D. Appleton-Century, 1932),
pp. 8, 9, 16. See also David K. Berlo, The Process of Communication: An Introduction to Theory
and Practice (New York: Holt, Rinehart, and Win-
ston, 1960), p. 29; and Merrill R. Abbey, Communication in Pulpit and Parish (Philadelphia: Westminster Press, 1973), p. 27.

[2]An excellent treatment is given of this subject in Berlo, The Process of Communication, p. 29,
notes 3, 4, 5, and 6.

[3]Carter V. Good and Douglas E. Scates, Methods
of Research (New York: Appleton-Century-Crofts,
Inc., 1954), p. 275.

[4]B. B. Baxter, The Heart of the Yale Lectures
(Grand Rapids: Baker Book House, 1971 reprint.)

[5]Gaylord L. Lehman, "The Themes of Preaching in the Yale Lectures: 1900-1958," Unpublished Th. D. dissertation, Southern Baptist
Theological Seminary, Louisville, Kentucky, 1961.

[6]Leo T. Crismon, "Mullins Lectures," Encyclo-
pedia of Southern Baptists, Vol. II (Nashville:
Broadman Press, 1956), p. 930. See also the will
of Mrs. Isla May Mullins, dated 1935, in the Boyce
Library, Southern Baptist Theological Seminary.

[7]Joint Faculty Minutes, Southern Baptist Seminary, September 9, 1937 and December 5, 1939.

[8]These include the 1944 lectures of George
A. Buttrick, the 1948 lectures of John Mackay,
the 1956 lectures of Theodore F. Adams, the 1957
lectures of Paul Scherer, the 1962 lectures of
Henry Grady Davis, the 1963 lectures of Samuel

H. Miller, the 1964 lectures of Harold Cooke
Phillips, and the 1975 lectures of William Muehl.
While Dr. Buttrick's lectures are complete, they
are not available. Dr. Buttrick kindly loaned
me the set of lectures for my study; he prefers
that the manuscript not be made available for un-
restricted distribution. Actually, Paul Scherer's
1957 lectures were eventually published eight
years later, along with some of his sermons, in
the book, The Word God Sent.

[9]These include the lectures and sermons given
since 1960, with the exception of D. E. King's
1973 sermons.

[10]These include portions of the 1944 lectures
of George A. Buttrick, Review and Expositor, XL,
No. 2 (1943), pp. 151-166, and No. 3. pp. 279-295;
the 1945 lectures of Halford E. Luccock, Review
and Expositor, X.II, No. 3 (1945), pp. 255-265, and
No. 4, pp. 383-392; the 1946 lectures of H. H.
Farmer, Review and Expositor, XLIII, No. 3 (1946),
pp. 243-260, No. 4. pp. 403-418, and XLIV, No. 1
(1947), pp. 34-49; the 1948 lectures of John A.
Mackay, Review and Expositor, XLVI, No. 1 (1949),
pp. 3-12; the 1957 lectures of Paul Scherer, Review
and Expositor, LIV, No. 3 (1957), pp. 355-66, No.
4, pp. 560-73.

[11]These include the 1952 lectures of T. W.
Manson. His lectures were entitled, "Some Aspects
of the Public Ministry of Our Lord." The sub-
title of his 1953 book is similar: The Servant-
Messiah: A Study of the Public Ministry of Jesus
(Grand Rapids: Baker Book House, 1977 reprint).
The 1954 lectures of David A. MacLennan have been
published as Pastoral Preaching (Philadelphia:
The Westminster Press, 1955). Robert J. McCracken's
1955 lectures form the substance of his book, The
Making of the Sermon (New York: Harper and Bros.,
1956). The 1961 lectures of Horton Davies comprise
chapter 10 of Worship and Theology in England: From

<u>Newman to Martineau, 1850-1900</u>, "Worship and The-
ology in England, " Vol. 4 (Princeton: Princeton
University Press, 1962). Joseph Sittler's 1966
lectures are in his book, <u>The Anguish of Preaching</u>
(Philadelphia: Fortress Press, 1967).

[12]These series were the 1947 sermons of Charles
L. Graham, the 1967 sermons of Elam Davis, the 1968
sermons of J. P. Allen, the 1969 sermons of Jack
Finegan, the 1972 sermons of Edmund Steimle, and
the 1973 sermons of D. E. King.

[13]The lectures not available include those of
William Lyon Phelps, given in 1942, the 1947 ser-
mons of Charles L. Graham, the 1949 lectures of
Elmer G. Homrighausen, the 1953 lectures of Harold
Cooke Phillips, the 1958 lectures of Clarence W.
Cranford, and the 1973 sermons of D. E. King.

CHAPTER II

THE SPEAKER

Aristotle dealt extensively with the matter of the speaker in his <u>Rhetoric</u>.[1] For the purpose of this study, the speaker is treated with reference to his being the preacher of a Christian congregation. The issues of his personality, preparation, and attitudes are explored. The use of the word "his" does not exclude women, but is used only as a convenient third person singular pronoun.

PERSONALITY

Who is the preacher? Donald Macleod has said that this is <u>the</u> question facing ministers today.[2] Macleod noted that the preacher must deal adequately with his own personality before he can deal with the Gospel. If he fails to do so, not only his preaching but also his ministry as a whole will fail. The man or woman who aspires to be a preacher needs to be aware of himself or herself as a unique individual, and above all, as a person.

Macleod said that preaching as an approved mode of communication seems to be on the wane.[3] Two typical responses are given to explain this degeneration. First, some say that the preacher himself is no longer seen as a knowledgeable person. His preaching no longer draws the great crowds. Second, the preacher is given lower status even within the church and its institutions. In the seminary, teachers of homiletics are treated as academic "retreads," men not quite up to par with the others on the theological faculty. Within denominational circles, the preacher is seen as a means of achieving program ends. On the parish front, the preacher/pastor is turned into an organizational man, thus becoming a pastor/director.

Both of these reasons are partially true, said Macleod, but one major reason stands behind the waining of preaching. "The basic disease is with the minister who has himself lost faith in preaching. Preaching has failed because the preacher has failed."[4] Thus, the crisis in preaching today is bound up with who the preacher himself is. Macleod asked, "Is the contemporary preacher sure of who he is and what his job is?"[5] If not, the conclusion is clear: "Whenever the preacher loses a sense of his true identity ... then what he says and what he stands for ceases to count."[6] Following Bishop Quale's dictum, Macleod noted that in the last analysis, preaching is <u>not</u> the making of a sermon and delivering it--it is the making of a preacher and delivering that.[7]

All of this points to the conclusion that the preacher's personality, who he is in relation to himself, God, and his people, is of utmost importance. His entire being is involved in the message he proclaims. Nothing of himself is left out.[8] Macleod used H. H. Farmer's concept of the preacher as being a "servant of the Word." "To be servant of the Word means that the preacher so gives himself to others that the . . . redemptive word in and through him might be formed in them."[9] "The Christ happening must be made present again through the living voice."[10]

George A. Buttrick also has said that the personality of the man preaching is of tremendous importance. He developed his idea in the following manner:

The chosen purpose of preaching is clear: it is to make known the good news so that men may believe it and be saved. The question then becomes: Is preaching the proper tool for <u>that</u> purpose?[11]
. . . .
Of all quickly available media, speech is the most adaptable, the most resilient, the

14

most weighted with meaning. It is quicker
than music or pageantry, more expressive
than signs or books. Words are instant:
they are almost inevitable. Nay, more:
they are the very breath of personality.
They are almost an incarnation of the man.[12]
. . . .
His energy is not merely in personality
through speech, or even in unassailable
axioms. It is in the axiom; that is, in the
Gospel, which is more than axiom.[13]

Buttrick climaxed his argument by stating: "So
the preacher, becoming one with the Gospel, becomes
one with its power."[14] Wishing to pursue the matter
further, however, he said,

If God would have direct dealings with
us into redemption, He must plead with us
as a man. If his incarnation is to be made
known, that proclamation (because it tells
the good news of the Incarnation) must be
through a man speaking to men. Therein is
preaching power.[15]

The preacher's personality is so bound up
in what he does and says that he can spoil the
Gospel because of a defect in personality.[16] On
the other hand, a healthy personality is a great
benefit. Said Buttrick, "The power of Christian
preaching is that he (the preacher) can speak as
a whole man with a whole voice . . . ."[17]

For the Christian preacher, personality is
not an item in vacuum. Instead, it is a facet
of his life which is itself transformed by God.
As Buttrick has insisted, "If the man himself has
not been found of God through the Gospel, he cannot
proclaim the good news to his neighbors."[18]

Robert J. McCracken has said, with regard
to personality, the preacher must give careful
attention to preparing his sermons, but ". . . it
is even more essential that he should prepare himself."[19] McCracken spoke here of preparation pursuant to a man's personality. Similar comments

have been made by John Claypool. He said that
the preacher must deal with his own personality
and makeup so as not to be constantly competing
with other ministers.[20] He must not look at
his work as a way of earning self-worth or of just-
ifying his profession.

The considerations above point out that the
personality of the preacher affects his work and
his effectiveness. The Mullins lecturers dealt
with a second aspect of the speaker-- his qualifications.

QUALIFICATIONS

The men who have dealt with the matter of the
qualifications of the preacher have said some powerful, if not shocking, things. For example, Samuel H. Miller has said that "ministers are called
to be saints."[21] By "saint" Miller meant one
who has had a deep personal experience with God,
and who continues that relationship. This relationship makes the preacher perceptive. Miller
put it in these terms:

> The minister is one forever on the look-
> out for revelation, keen to discover the little
> epiphanies of God amid the commonplace events
> of ordinary men, tiptoe to see the glory
> which shines now and then in the soul of a
> nobody. When he sees it, he should know how
> to celebrate it in prayer and praise, choos-
> ing just the right words, the right images,
> so that men's faith stands confirmed and
> their joy is made perfect.[22]

Awareness of God

The preacher's entire life is to be imbued
with his sense of God's reality. James McCord
said that the preacher must learn to live and
think theologically.[23] God will be ever present
with him, fulfilling this qualification of awareness and experience.

16

H. Grady Davis has said that this awareness of God is noticeable.

> The primary question is whether the people will hear anybody besides the preacher, or will hear only a man talking. If somebody other than he is the really important speaker, that sets an entirely new standard of the sermon. In that case, the decisive thing is not the sermon's quality as the self-expression of a good, religious man. The decisive thing is the sermon's quality as a medium through which the voice of that Other may be heard.[24]

Davis noted the shift toward the transcendent element in preaching, especially since about 1930. Before that time, homiletical literature treated preaching as merely the activity and self-expression of a good man.[25]

God-Changed

Theodore F. Adams emphasized the importance of the preacher being one who has experienced a God-caused change in his life.[26] This change keeps him from mere "professionalism," which is "the relying on the conventional forms instead of seeking for the substance beneath."[27] Coupled with this emphasis on the minister being changed is an assertion that this God-caused change gives the preacher his authority. Dr. Claypool said the secret of powerful preaching is for the preacher to let the truth which has found him become true witness to others.[28] "The preacher's ultimate authority is always personal experience."[29] Claypool asserted:

> One of the problems is that so much of our preaching has just been the transmission of abstract truth that has never become existentially real to the preacher, and therefore has little power in terms of the one who hears.
> . . . .
> What has spoken home to my heart has the

17

best chance of speaking home to the heart
of another.[30]

Claypool went on to say in that lecture that the
God-like quality within the preacher, caused by
his experience of God, is the source of both
authority and power.

Identification with People

The preacher must closely identify with his
people. This is the only way that he can truly
speak to them. Doing so in not always easy, however. As Theodore F. Adams has noted, "Ministers
are, in a very real sense, protected from life,
and need to recognize that fact."[31] Further, "We
are insulated to a certain degree from some areas
of life."[32] This being so, said Adams, the preacher
is under obligation to keep his finger on the pulse
of his people, to know them intimately, and to
identify with their problems.

This identification requires the minister to
have a life of culture, according to H. H. Farmer.[33]
By "culture" Farmer meant breadth of learning and
experience. This is the only thing which allows
him truly to identify with his congregation and
yet not be dragged down in his own faith. Farmer
said that the minister must ask himself how he
is going to face frankly and realistically all
the "muck and misery, the tragedy and heartbreak,
the agony and frustration of human life and yet
find his sensitivity to high things . . not only
not impaired, but also growing stronger."[34] Thus,
the preacher is not to identify with people to
the point of losing his own faith and his ability
to help others.

The preacher can identify with his people
further by trying to understand what the Gospel
does in his life, and therefore what it can do
in his people's lives. H. Grady Davis has put it
in the following terms:

18

We can see the gospel's relevance to ourselves, the people in the pews, in the towns
and suburbs of America, in all areas of this
frightened world. Once we have seen its relevance for ourselves, we can learn how to spell
it out in the concrete particulars of contemporary human existence.
. . . .
All our anxious concerns over the frustrating
problems of communication, the treacherous
character of language, semantics--all this shows
that we can not speak to our contemporaries
in general.[35]

All of this betrays a false view of preaching,
said Davis. He asked:

What is this way of preaching? It is a
speech about religious ideas and practices,
about some theological questions perhaps,
maybe about the Bible or God or Jesus, cer-
tainly about us some ethical or moral issue,
some personal problem or possibility. It is
a man talking about such things.
. . . .
But if, as we believe, God in Christ is present here in the church service, if he is now
speaking to us for Himself by his Spirit,
giving his own command and making his personal
promise, and if he is doing this in the text
of holy scripture, then preaching is a different thing entirely, and it has to be done in
a very different way.
. . . .
It is the preacher's business to put the text
in the middle of life, where he and his people are living, and let it speak for itself
to both him and them together.[36]

Davis is adamant in his insistence that the preacher be close to his people, but that he take
care not to allow his own beliefs and preaching
be swallowed up in their opinions.

Man of Conviction

The preacher is to possess the qualification of conviction and courage. This intrepidity removes the preacher from the charge leveled against him that he is merely a minion of his congregation's wishes. Kelley Miller Smith said that courage is the distinctive mark of black preachers in American history.[37] All ministers, not just black ones, need conviction and courage.

John A. Mackay has noted that without the authority given by strong conviction, the preacher's words will have no force to get through to secular men.[38]

Now I venture to say that there's nobody in academic circles, or popular circles today, who is going to make the slightest impression or the slightest impact on the thought, life or programs of people unless those who listen to him get the impression that the man has convictions. Nobody is going to make "first base" today who does not represent a tremendous conviction.[39]

Mackay pointed out that people always flocked to hear Reinhold Niebuhr speak, not because they agreed with him, but because they knew that he truly believed what he said.

The preacher must not be diffident in his ideas, actions, or even the very words used to form the sermon. Said Mackay,

The words that we use in many a sermon, and the concepts, are simply not understood by the people, or they are understood so well by the people that they have a sopheric [sic] effect on the people, and they go to sleep. They are so used to certain words and phrases that they do not make the slighest impression anymore. Now a new preacher appears and there

20

may be questions here and there, but if they
hear one or two classical words, "blood,"
"grace," etc., then "that preacher is all
right."[40]

Thus, the preacher must never be a sycophant,
seeking only to "please" his congregation. He
must not inveigle them with pet phrases which
sound orthodox but carry little meaning. The
question may be raised, "How can the preacher
develop and retain such strong convictions without being forced by the pressures of his parish
to relinquish them?" H. H. Farmer helped to
answer this question in his 1946 Mullins lectures.[41] Convictions, said Farmer, come as an
outgrowth of a strong spiritual and intellectual
life. There is a close relationship between
cultural life of a minister and the quality of
his personal life as a Christian man.[42] His
culture, that is his breadth of knowledge and
experience, is linked together with his convictions. As this culture grows, so does the
preacher's religious life, and concomitantly,
so do his personal convictions and courage.
Self-descipline, self-purification, and self-
enlargement are bound up together and all play
an important role in establishing and main-
taining the minister's ideas.

He is put into a dilemma, however, with the
temptation being to compromise his beliefs.
Farmer said that the preacher partially can
escape this temptation by imbibing the ideas
of great thinkers of all ages.[43] This action
helps the minister to be intransigent in his
convictions, but responsive to the thoughts and
needs of his people. "A mature and strong Christian soul is at once ruthlessly frank and sincere
in facing evil and corruption and yet at the
same time most sensitively responsive to what is
good."[44] Farmer noted that because ministers
and Protestantism in general failed to offer a
Christian humanism to people, that is, an intelligent and aesthetic view of life, false humanisms

21

emerged.[45]

The minister must be courageous in his
preaching. No one better pointed out this fact
than did William Muehl. He said that the preacher
must boldly conceptualize God's activity in the
world and preach that fact vigorously.[46]

To speak effectively of what it means to
say that God is now as in the beginning first
and above all the Creator--one must be prepared to acknowledge that God does not regard
human pain as the ultimate evil, that it is
not the lash with which he afflicts the un-
faithful--but that suffering is a complex
phenomenon, as complex as the God whose pur-
posing will it serves in diverse ways.[47]

Moral Purity

The minister is to lead a morally pure life.
This assertion was taken for granted by most of
the lecturers, for they said little about it.
Several exceptions do exist, however. G. Earl
Guinn quoted John Baillie as saying, "Even Christ
had to remind himself that His ministry to men
could not bear proper fruit unless he saw to it
first that his own life was holy."[48] Guinn concluded that "the minister must be holy for the
sake of those to whom he would minister. There
is no mixture that smells so rank to heaven and
so offends the nostrils of men as a religion that
is hypocritical."[49]

A cultural difference is important to note
here. Kelley Miller Smith has said that for
black preachers the issue of personal morality
is subordinated to their ability to preach
effectively and vigorously.[50] Smith's comment
notwithstanding, personal morality was posited
as a sine qua non in the life of the preacher.

PREPARATION

The term "preparation" here refers to the

22

training and equipping of the preacher himself, and not the preparation of the sermon. Examined here are the views of the lecturers in regard to personal preparation and education.

Robert J. McCracken has said that long before the preacher thinks of beginning work on a sermon "it is even more essential that he should prepare himself."[51] He went on to say that such preparation is a life-long process.

> If we do not give heed to the enrichment of character, if with the passage of the years we do not acquire personal weight . . . it matters little how eloquent we may be as preachers, our ministry will always convey to the discerning the impression that we lack something vital and indispensable.[52]

McCracken further asserted that personal preparation requires attention to two areas of ministerial life. The first is the great themes of the Bible.

> To deal with the pivotal themes of the Evangel, to "take heed unto the doctrine," we must keep on subjecting ourselves to a vigorous self-discipline. But if we do it we shall, in the words of Scriptures, save ourselves as well as our hearers.[53]

The second area of attention deals with a preacher's preparation in reference to his congregation. McCracken said, "Cultivate the shepherd heart. Be a conscientious visitor and pastor. Never lose the human touch."[54] Further, "There is a close connection between pastoral work and pulpit work. Fidelity in one may lead to outstanding power and usefulness in the other."[55]

The Seminary

The seminary has much to do with the preparation of a person for ministry. James I.

McCord, President of Princeton Theological Seminary, has said that a seminary has three goals concerning students.[56] First, it helps them think theologically. Second, the seminary assists the student in the acquisition of as broad a theological culture as possible. Third, the seminary enables the theologue to become an ongoing participant in the entire theological enterprise. On the whole, McCord spoke highly of the usefulness of the seminary is a minister's preparation.

This high view was not shared by Joseph Sittler, however. As Sittler expressed it, "There seems to be no correlation at all between excellence of formalized theological studies and lively preaching of the Word of God."[57] In trying to explain the reason for this gap, Sittler gave several answers. The transference from seminary to sermon does happen sometimes, but not often.

More typical is the sermon that remains trapped in its own starting point, meaningful only within that segment of history that provided its text or pericope, and effective in the illumination of only that situation which was its accidental occasion. Biblical reportage of mighty events remains a sort of verbal iconography, a celebration of godly vitality that remains unpunctured for explosion into the present.

. . . .

The gap between the magnificence of the Christian substance and the palid and pulpy content of the parish sermon can only be narrowed if we radically redefine the relation of church and school, grant to the school what belongs to her by charter, and hold her accountable in terms appropriate to her function.[58]

Sittler went on to explicate his thesis with

24

reference to institutionalism.

The profoundest reason for the prevailing
low level of transference of theological culture to sermonic force lies in the dynamics of
an organizational ethos. The preacher shares
the human disposition to perform at the level
required by man's expectations and demands.
The prevailing mood in the contemporary congregation does not make those expectations high
or those demands strict.
. . . .
The church, in the most visible mode of her
existence in the world, is institution, and
institution and investigation have always sustained an understandable but lamentable sus-
picion of one another. The church as institi-
tution is always tempted to view the school
as the formal bearer of its portfolio of
doctrine and procedural stock and to assign
it the function to train purveyors of the same.
From this expectation it arises that so many
students enter our schools with no clear promise or intention to engage in rigorous re-
enactment and fresh command of theological
culture, but rather with the intention of
being provided with retailing competence as
dispensers of a solidified and frequently
uncriticized churchly wholesale product.59

Building upon this foundation, Sittler went on to
make his boldest statement about the seminary
and its role in preparing persons to preach.

Preaching is an act of the church in which
the substance of her faith is ever seen
freshly declared and reinterpreted to a level
of men who live within the instant and changing actuality of history. And, therefore,
any stylization or theoretical absolution
of the correct relation between seminary instruction and the task of preaching must be

25

resisted. And, therefore, the expectation must not be cherished that, save for modest and obvious instruction about voice, pace, organization, and such matters, preaching as a lively art of the church can be taught at all.[60]

This is true, said Sittler, because preaching is an intellectual and creative function of faith-substance in motion within a concrete circumstance.[61] If preaching is not so understood, then all "efforts to improve it by special discipline serve only to solidify our error."[62] For Sittler, the role of the seminary in preparing the preacher is, at best, ambiguous. He is not sure what it can do for the young theologue, especially in light of his conclusion. "The student in his preaching commonly remains determined by the model or models he knew before he came to seminary."[63]

Art

Samuel Miller has said that the preacher should use art to prepare himself.[64] Art, said Miller, helps the preacher increase his perception and awareness. It gives him new insights into the nature of reality. Miller put it in the following terms:

And if the minister has no vision of reality, and if he has not been initiated into anything deeper than the ordinary sequence of happenstance, if he has not blundered or broken through the limits of this all too present world into the realm of reality, where the foundations cannot be shaken and things are everlasting, then he is not merely poor, he is pathetic, a clown with a make-believe sceptre.[65]

Miller wanted to know why preachers are taught to use words in order to be precise and powerful in their testimony regarding the Word, but "completely

26

ignore their training in such images as would
enable them to transmit their vision of reality."[66]

Ministers ransack literature and do everything they can do to increase their vocabulary;
why not ransack art and do everything we can
to develop our perceptiveness? Why does there
seem to be such a vast gulf fixed between the
man who listens and the man who looks, between
the speaker and the seer? Did God not make the
eye even as he made the tongue?
. . . .
. . . great art has a religious function, and
without it the minister is impoverished for
lack of means to communicate the profound
vision of reality which lies at the heart
of faith.[67]

Quoting George Bernard Shaw, Miller summed up
his argument as follows: "You use a mirror to
see your face; you use works of art to see your
soul."[68]

ATTITUDES

The attitudes which the preacher possesses
will shape his entire ministry, for good or ill.
Several of the lecturers have dealt with this
aspect of the preacher's life.

Catholicity

Harold Cooke Phillips has said that three
facets of the preacher's faith always must be
kept in focus.[69] First, there is the gospel's
view of God--dynamic, but unified. Second, there
is the gospel's view of man--sinful, but with
hope in Christ. Third, there is the gospel's
view of history--moving, but not circular. Held
together, there three truths force the minister
to keep his eyes on the world larger than his
own parish.

27

Said Phillips:

> The preacher is not the chaplain of a private
> club. The problems of the world must be in
> our minds, its needs on our hearts. If not,
> our God is too small. The "hot gospel" which
> ignores our involvement in the total life of
> man is not hot, nor ever warm; it is frozen
> stiff![70]

Donald Macleod echoed some of these same feelings
in his 1970 lectures. He said that the minister
gets into trouble if his attitude toward ministry
is that of the "lone ranger," that is, one who
does his work in isolation.[71]

Professional

The preacher is to be a professional in that
he is thorough, careful, and competent. But as
Roger Fredrikson has observed, the minister must
move beyond the attitude of a "professionalism,"
that is, looking at the ministry as an eight-to-
five, five-day-a-week "job."[72] Fredrikson said
that obedience to God is the key to being truly
professional in the ministry.

Donald Macleod has outlined four reasons why
ministers have failed to be professionals.[73]
1. They possess a parochial view of preaching.
2. They are too conscious of numbers, budgets,
   and other concrete realities.
3. They succumb to the boredom of the middle
   years.
4. They lose their souls by becoming program
   oriented.

Existential Involvement

The minister is to allow the gospel to possess
him, to be existentially involved in the entire
process of ministry. Joseph Sittler used the act

23

of preaching as a paradigm for all ministry.

   Preaching is not merely something a preacher
does; it is a function of the preacher's
whole existence concentrated at the point of
declaration and interpretation. The act of
preaching is organic to the placement of the
man himself as believer, doubter, sinner,
aspirer; organic to the rich magnitude of the
historical life of the catholic church in such
a way as both to illuminate the particularity
of this time, this place, this people--and to
gather that particularity up into the prodigious
pattern of the past.[74]

SUMMARY

   This chapter has looked at the preacher,
his personality, qualifications, preparation,
and attitudes. The identity of the preacher,
who he is as a person, greatly affects his work
and shapes his thought. It exists in relationship to other persons and has interaction with
them. The preacher's qualifications include
a God-changed life, a constant awareness of God,
identification with people, possession of strong
convictions, and moral purity. Preparation
of the preacher includes the preparation of himself personally, his seminary training, and his
use of art to increase his awareness. The preacher's attidudes shape his ministry and have to do
with his conduct of his work as a professional
and his existential involvement in his work.

[1]The Rhetoric of Aristotle, translated by
Lane Cooper (New York: D. Appleton-Century,
1932), pp. 1, et passim.

[2]Donald Macleod, in a lecture ("The Identity
of the Preacher") at the Southern Baptist Theological Seminary, Louisville, Kentucky, March,
1970 (tape on file at Boyce Library Audio-
Visual Center.)

[3]Macleod, in a lecture ("Crisis In Preaching")
at the Southern Baptist Theological Seminary,
March, 1970 (tape on file in the Boyce Library).

[4]Ibid.

[5]Ibid.

[6]Ibid.

[7]Macleod, "The Identity of the Preacher."

[8]Ibid.

[9]Ibid.

[10]Ibid.

[11]George A. Buttrick, "Power--And the Man,"
Review and Expositor, XL, No. 3, (1943), pp. 279-
295. I worked from Dr. Buttrick's original manuscript. The page numbers therefore refer to it.

[12]Ibid., pp. 5-6.

[13]Ibid., p. 11.

[14]Ibid., p. 12.

[15]Ibid., p. 13.

[16] Ibid., p. 15.

[17]Ibid., p. 21.

[18]Buttrick, "The Craftsmanship of the Preacher, (B)," (Louisville: Boyce Library, The Southern Baptist Theological Seminary, 1943), p. 17. (Mimeographed.)

[19]Robert J. McCracken, The Making of the Sermon (New York: Harper and Brothers, 1956), p. 10.

[20]John Claypool, in a lecture ("Preaching and the Preacher") at The Southern Baptist Theological Seminary, March, 1974 (tape on file at Boyce Library).

[21]Samuel H. Miller, "The Insight of Saints-- And Morals" (Louisville: Boyce Library, The Southern Baptist Theological Seminary, 1963), p. 1 (Mimeographed.)

[22]Ibid., p. 15.

[23]James McCord, in a lecture (unnamed, but fourth in a series) at The Southern Baptist Theological Seminary, March, 1977 (tape on file at Boyce Library).

[24]H. Grady Davis, "The Personal Word" (Louisville: Boyce Library, The Southern Baptist Theological Seminary, 1962), p. 8 (Mimeographed).

[25]Ibid., p. 9.

[26]Theodore F. Adams, "The Preacher Looks at Himself and His People" (Louisville: Boyce Library, The Southern Baptist Theological Seminary, 1956), p. 4. (Mimeographed.)

[27]Ibid. See also another lecture in that same series, "The Faith of a Preacher," p. 3.

[28]John Claypool, in a lecture ("The Authority of the Preacher") at The Southern Baptist Theological Seminary, March, 1974 (tape on file at the Boyce Library).

[29]Ibid.

[30]Ibid.

[31]Adams, op. cit., p. 10.

[32]Ibid., pp. 10-11.

[33]H. H. Farmer, "The Preacher and Culture," Review and Expositor, XLIV, No. 1, (1947), p. 37.

[34]Ibid.

[35]H. Grady Davis, "The Contemporary Word" (Louisville: Boyce Library, The Southern Baptist Theological Seminary, 1962), pp. 18-20. (Mimeographed.)

[36]Ibid., pp. 21-23.

[37]Kelley Miller Smith, in a lecture ("Through a Glass Blackly") at The Southern Baptist Theological Seminary, March, 1971 (tape on file at Boyce Library).

[38]John Mackay, "God's Unveiled Secret" (Louisville: Boyce Library, The Southern Baptist Theological Seminary, 1948), p. 43. (Mimeographed.)

[39] Ibid.

[40] Ibid., pp. 44-45.

[41] H. H. Farmer, "The Preacher and Culture,"
Review and Expositor, XLIV, No. 1 (1947),
pp. 34-49.

[42] Ibid., p. 36.

[43] Ibid., p. 39.

[44] Ibid., pp. 38-39.

[45] Ibid., p. 44.

[46] William Muehl, "The Height of Creativity"
(Louisville: Boyce Library, The Southern
Baptist Theological Seminary, 1974), p. 14.
(Mimeographed.)

[47] Ibid.

[48] G. Earl Guinn, quoting John Baillie,
"That the Ministry Might Not Be Ashamed" (Louis-
ville: Boyce Library, The Southern Baptist
Theological Seminary, 1960). (Mimeographed.)

[49] Ibid.

[50] Smith, "Through a Glass Blackly."

[51] McCracken, The Making of the Sermon,
p. 10.

[52] Ibid., pp. 10-11.

[53] Ibid., p. 17.

[54] Ibid., p. 19.

[55] Ibid.

[56]James McCord, in a lecture ("The Anthropological Question") at The Southern Baptist Theological Seminary, March, 1977 (tape on file at Boyce Library).

[57]Joseph Sittler, The Anguish of Preaching (Philadelphia: Fortress Press, 1967), p. 4.

[58]Ibid., p. 4.

[59]Ibid., pp. 5-6.

[60]Ibid., p. 7.

[61]Ibid., p. 8.

[62]Ibid.

[63]Ibid., p. 9.

[64]Samuel Miller, "The Vision of Reality--And Art" (Louisville: Boyce Library, The Southern Theological Seminary, 1963), pp. 1-2. (Mimeographed.)

[65]Ibid., p. 2.

[66]Ibid.

[67]Ibid., p. 2, 5.

[68]Ibid., p. 5.

[69]Harold Cooke Phillips, "The Relevant Word" (Louisville: Boyce Library, The Southern Theological Seminary, 1964), pp. 2-7. (Mimeographed.)

[70]Ibid., p. 7.

[71]Donald Macleod, in a lecture ("Crisis in Preaching") at the Southern Baptist Theological Seminary, March, 1970 (tape on file at Boyce Library).

[72]Roger Fredrikson, in a lecture ("Look Who's Coming to the Party") at The Southern Baptist Theological Seminary, March, 1976 (tape on file at Boyce Library).

[73]Macleod, "Crisis in Preaching."

[74]Sittler, Anguish of Preaching, p. 8.

CHAPTER III

THE SPEECH

The second element in Aristotle's triad is the speech. In this case it refers specifically to the message, that is, the sermon. The concept of a sermon conveys two distinct ideas. The first is the <u>content</u> of the message. This content has to do with the essence of the sermon which is the Gospel itself. The second idea conveyed by the concept of a sermon is that of the <u>form</u> and <u>structure</u>. The first concept has to do with definitions of what a sermon is and what its sources are. The second deals with matters such as style, delivery, setting, and craftsmanship, thus establishing a sermon as a channel of communication.

CONTENT OF THE MESSAGE

Before the question, "What is a sermon?" can be answered, several background issues first must be explored. The content of the sermon must come first. This is actually a theological question. Since substance precedes form, the theological issues behind the form must be considered.

The Gospel

In a lecture entitled, "What Is The Gospel?", George Buttrick tried to give a theological rationale for the act of preaching.[1]

> Good news, by its nature . . . is something that has happened. It is an <u>event</u> breathtaking in surprise and joy. The Gospel is a work so blessed that it taxes belief and shakes the soul in sobs of gladness.
> . . . .

Preaching is not the airing of our opinions
on books or history or even Jesus. It is
not a lecture on religion. It is not the
"Christian interpretation of life," but
the declaration of an event, without which
there could be no Christian interpretation
of life. It is not a proclamation (in
initial instance) of Christian faith, but
of that thrust-into-history which only
could quicken Christian faith. The verb,
to preach, means, to herald. The Gospel
is the heralding of something already done
for man, the annunciation of a fact . . . .[2]

Buttrick also noted that "The Gospel is an
accomplished fact: 'The Word became flesh and
dwelt among us.' Preaching is the heralding of
that ever-present, ever-living fact."[3] H. Grady
Davis agreed with Buttrick's contention that the
Gospel and its proclamation are inextricably
bound together. Davis said:

The preaching of the gospel is itself
part of God's deed in Christ, an event in
the redeeming work of God in Christ. That
is to say, that the death and resurrection
of Jesus Christ and their being preached
next Sunday morning in your pulpit, are
parts of the same act of that love with
which God so loved the world.[4]

Two other lecturers have dealt extensively
with the concept of "Gospel" in their lectures.
These are Paul Scherer and William Muehl. Scherer's views are considered first.

Scherer began by insisting that if preaching
were again to become a radical transaction, that
is, a costly affair, then "we have to take
serious account of the conflicts which the gospel
provokes, of the claims with which it confronts
us, and of whatever possibilities there are on
our part of creative response."[5] Three things
follow from this assertion. First, the gospel

comes, not as history, but as conflict. Second,
it comes, not only as succor, but also as
demand. Third, the gospel comes, not as refuge,
but as creative response.[6] All of this means
that the Gospel lays heavy demands upon persons
and is not merely an avenue of escaping respon-
sible living. This costliness keeps the Gospel
from being cheap and the pulpit from being
"cowards castle." Scherer noted that:

> The Christian pulpit in America has been
> mightily busy reducing the cost of the
> Christian faith and of the Christian life.
> What God did cost him all he had; one
> reads nowhere in the New Testament that
> the cost for us has been marked down
> . . . .[7]

The gospel creates new situations. "It doesn't
play second fiddle to any problem: It's the
concert-master! It's the conductor that sets
the problems! It's the composer that writes
the score!"[8]

> The gospel, as the basis of the sermon,
> carries with it three notes of authenticity.
> The first is _authority_. "Nothing can happen--
> and every time we preach something should
> happen--if the note of authority is missing,"
> said Scherer.[9] He developed his thesis as
> follows below:

> We begin with the knowledge that the
> problems of living are one thing; the
> problems of life are another! Preach-
> ing has that for its business, and so
> does the gospel. Not as an emphasis,
> but as a center of gravity. The preach-
> er's ultimate vantage-point, the only
> authority he has which is final, stems
> from that place where in the presence
> of God the problems of living become
> the problems of life, and of the Word
> that confronts it.

. . . .

Because the Bible, and preaching that's
truly Biblical, are both of them places
of meeting between God and the human
soul, the sermon doesn't always have
to be introduced with a story. It isn't
necessary, or even desirable, to stir up
some fictitious and transitory interest;
then, when you think you have them fooled
into paying attention, try to arrange a
carryover into the real subject matter!
Better to start at once by touching some
vital nerve which the Bible itself exposes!
And by the same token, the conclusion
doesn't always have to be a summary! [10]

Still dealing with authority as one of three
authentic marks of the gospel, Scherer went
on to say that this authority is mediated
through carefully chosen words and phrases
in preaching. He urged the preacher to take
to expository preaching,

    . . . not just of poor, lonely, extir-
pated texts, but of whole sections and
passages, not broken up, verse by verse,
but whole, that the Bible may have a
chance to preach itself! Perhaps that
way you can contribute to some new understanding of Christian doctrine in an age
philosophically and metaphysically bank-
rupt! I think it was Hugh Thompson Kerr
of Princeton who recently pointed out
that the theological vocabulary of the
Bible is rooted in the experience of shop-
girl and garage mechanic, husband and wife,
politician and derelict in the gutter. All
of this means, among other things, that you
will not be bogging down in history, or
reducing faith to intuition or aspiration,
morals to ideals, salvation to going to

heaven, and the will of God to principles
of law. The world is sufficiently de-
personalized as it is, you will not be
helping it along! It means that you will
not forever be proving something that
can't be proved, or setting forth con-
ceptual and propositional truth as if
that came first, doling out a great deal
of information about God, or giving a
lecture on repentence, or on Christianity as a philosophy or way of life. It
means that you will be posing the risks
we take in prayer, in worship, in commit-
ment; intellectual risks, moral risks,
without trying to maneuver people into
the Kingdom of God, or subverting their
freedom as persons. It means that you
will be exploring for yourself the realities that we call faith, and hope, and
love, filling them with content again,
eschewing the "language of Zion," but not
its elemental speech; analyzing and defin-
ing your words until you have succeeded in
saying that they mean, and what he meant
who used them there on the pages of Scripture.[11]

Scherer added this final word as it related to
the gospel and its authority.

It derives ultimately not from but
through the words of Scripture, and is will-
ing to tabernacle in your own; but it trans-
cends them all, establishing itself beyond
the words in the Word which God speaks.
It has very little to do with infallibility,
as we often define it. It has to do with
a Person, and the persons to whom the
living Christ reveals and imparts himself.
There is its source, in him whose only
answer to the world is what it was before:
"Neither tell I you by what authority I do
these things." The Word of God does not
label itself. Sunsets are not signed. It
asserts itself. It is the cutting edge of
God's Kingdom.[12]

Authority, therefore, is the first element of authenticity of the gospel, according to Paul Scherer. The second element is <u>urgency</u>. The concept of eschatology means that all time is God-filled time, and this adds the note of urgency. Scherer wondered how preaching ever could become a routine business. "The sermon doesn't address itself to a crisis; it creates a crisis; and all at once something has to be done, as between the shadow of death and the promise of life."[13]

Added to authority and urgency is the note of <u>triumph</u> in the gospel. Scherer said that this element is often missing from many sermons, but that it should always be there. "The Christian sermon is the sign of that certainty which sees in the very moment of confusion that the tragedy is not central. The triumph is."[14]

Building upon his preceding argument, Scherer went on to talk about the credibility and relevance of the gospel.[15] Following the ideas of H. H. Farmer, Scherer noted that many people feel that the gospel is incredible, irrelevant, and cheap. He paraphrased R. Gregor Smith and explained what he meant by "Gospel." Concerning the gospel, Scherer said that it

is not merely a message about the world, or man, or God, which it wishes to get across . . . . Its message is a combina- tion of a message with a messenger. It concentrates this unique effort in what is called the Word. The message of Christianity is words plus the bringer of the words, it is the teaching and the teacher, it is an intellectual content claiming to be truth, along with a living Being claiming to be the living truth. The world of thought and the world of existence come together in this unique identity called the Word of God. The two worlds are not seen as an amalgam, nor as a combination to be grasped in two

successive movements. But they are seen
as one; not the message and then the
messenger, nor one without the other; but
both together, in one, the living Word.[16]

For Scherer, the gospel is the apex of meeting
between God and the human soul. The preacher
therefore cannot merely urge people to "go to
church because you will feel better. They may
feel worse!"[17]

The charge that the gospel is "incredible"
involves two things. First, it is presented as
being less or other than what it is. Second,
". . . the preacher has allowed the tragic sense
of life to slip out of it."[18] Scherer asked
what kind of preaching makes the gospel seem too
small. He concluded that it is the kind in which

beatitudes are turned into platitudes, glit-
tering generalities, over-simplifications,
fifty-seven different ways to wrap life up
into neat bundles tied with a ribbon. What
we preach may seem incredible, far too small
to be true, because it's shallow. Take
everything you say and hold it up before the
toughest lot you can imagine, the hardest
road, the most agonizing need, and see how
it looks there!

. . . .

We need to be rescued from the too cozy
optimism of the Pollyanna sermon, with
something on every page to be thankful
about, especially on the last page. Even
the conclusion has to be something other
than the grin of the Cheshire cat which
remains behind when the cat was gone! Not
that we are called on to be lugubrious and
sombre. God forbid! Paul never was! But
surely every preacher is supposed to know
something of the shadows that keep stealing
across the sunlight of human existence.

43

The only pattern the sunlight makes is
with the shadow it throws![19]

Scherer concluded that, in the gospel, triumph
and tragedy are just too intertwined to be
unraveled. The apostle Paul "got excited about
the way things _were_ in the teeth of the way
things _looked_! He got excited about the sheer
effrontery of the gospel!"[20]

The second charge leveled at the gospel is
that it is simply "irrelevant." Scherer con-
ceded this charge to be true if "what is
preached seems too _confident_ to be true."[21] The
real "offence" of the gospel does not lie in its
miracles; its real offence lies in its persistent
upsetting of "even our religious apple-carts!
It's not with what we _like_, but what we _don't_
like that we have to come to grips!"[22] For this
reason, sermons which try to solve complex difficulties with shallow answers, and which try
only to ease life's burdens, are not likely to
have a deep and lasting significance.

Is it that we make the gospel seem irrelevant when we allow the offence of the gospel
to disappear in the effort to preach something that will be helpful and so spend our
time announcing too confidently what is
itself too confident to be true? You can't
be helpful without disturbing anybody. You
can't do people good without stirring them
out of their complacency. They have never
heard the gospel until they have been made
uneasy by it: until they have ferreted out,
in every case, not so much what it is that
pleases them as what it is that offends
them.[23]

The third charge is that the gospel is
cheap. Scherer insisted that a "goody-good" God
could be nothing for us. Yet many pulpits have
marked down the price of the gospel's demand
upon us. "The shaking of the foundations at

Easter has been reduced to the rocking of a cradle (of Christmas), its blinding light to pastel shades!"[24] Preachers must first recognize the costliness of grace in their own lives and then let it cut through to their hearers' hearts.

Another person who dealt extensively with the concept of the gospel is William Muehl. He pointed out that the use of a manuscript in preaching disturbs some people because it symbolizes for them the possibility that "there may be more to Christian faith than can be fully communicated in simple declarative sentences."[25]

Here, in my mind, is one of the greatest obstacles to effective preaching in American Protestant churches in our time. The widespread and deeply rooted assumption, even on the part of the highly educated, sophisticated men and women, that there is an inescapable and proper correlation between simplicity and truth in religious discourse. People who would not dream of turning to the Reader's Digest for definitive information about law, education, politics, sex, business, or just any other important aspect of their lives--look to just sources for the last word about God.[26]

This view sets up a false alternative, however. It seems to say that the gospel must come forth as either "spiritual pabulum" or as "abstruse and irrelevant theological lectures." This assumption is built upon a lie--"the insistence upon quick and easy answers to the massive complexity of our relationship with God."[27]

People establish wholly artificial ground rules for religious discourse, set up artificial intellectual limits which make true communication impossible--and then condemn the preacher for being merely a nice little man who cannot face the facts of life--and

45

blush at their own folly in even pretend-
ing to take his message seriously. And I
suggest that the purposes of evil are
served far better by such a strategy than
by all the pornographic movies ever made.
Because it enables us to define religion
as irrelevant to life. And gives us the
perfect excuse to ignore the counsels of
religion.[28]

This oversimplification radically alters the
impact of the gospel and its place as the basis
of the sermon. Muehl said that this rejection
"has made it exceedingly difficult for the
pulpit to address seriously the complicated
forms in which the dilemmas of the human spirit
present themselves in a rapidly changing world."[29]
He developed his argument in the following manner:

It is the proper job of the preacher so to
proclaim the gospel that it will have obvious and salutory challenges which all of us
face from day to day. Now when the man or
woman in the pulpit is committed by the
folklore of simplistic Protestantism to
say nothing that might tax the mind--when
he or she is bound to some a priori assumption that the will of God can always be
stated in Sunday School terms--the burden
of relevant preaching becomes almost impos-
sible to carry. No sane person expects the
preacher to have at his fingertips a detail-
ed blueprint of the moral life, one easily
applicable to the myriad variations with
which history confronts us. But what all
reasonable men and women do expect is that
the leadership of the pulpit will give some
evidence of understanding how complicated
true discipleship can be amid the conflicts
and tensions of a fallen world.[30]

Another problem with this oversimplification
is that it removes the mystery from the gospel.
Said Muehl:

One of the baneful legacies of the . . .
Reader's Digest doctrine of faith is the
idea that nothing be left mysterious, that
the . . . truth of any theological assertion is the degree to which it commends
itself to . . . common sense.[31]

To such an idea, Muehl responded as follows:

If it cannot be preached to the saving of
souls, it is not the gospel of Jesus Christ.
In religious terms persuasiveness is the
basic test of truth.

. . . .

All too frequently we seem to believe that
the art of homiletics consists of finding
the best words, metaphors, and analogies
with which to explain to the people in the
pews just what it is that the great minds
of theology have taught us. In other words,
the preacher is seen to be the recipient of
doctrinal insight, one who plays no active
part in formulating the substance of the
message.

. . . .

Didactic theology has all the answers. But
the preacher is the one who lives much closer
to the human heart. And because he is, he has
both the right and the obligation to preserve
the tension between academy and pulpit which
is so essential to the promulgation of a
saving gospel. I am suggesting, you see,
that it is quite wrong to speak as though
we have a message on the one hand and the
messenger on the other.[32]

Muehl summed up his thesis as follows:

It is error to suppose that theological
statement is the truth, waiting to be taught
and delivered in sermon. Truth is that
living action of God in Christ, ever present
in our lives, which theology looks at from

one side and preaching from another.
Neither has the truth. Both share in the
discovery and dissemination.[33]

Thus for Muehl, the gospel is not merely abstract
truth which is simply given in toto by the
preacher to his congregation. It is the dynamic
working of God in Christ. If that is not the
very essence of the message, then the message,
for whatever else it may be, is not a sermon.

The Word of God

Harold Cooke Phillips has reminded his
hearers that they must have a clear conception
of what the Word of God is in relation to the
content of their preaching.[34] Phillips said
that ministers today must realize that our
parents' questions are no longer our own. The
issue for the preacher is this: how to preach
the Eternal Word in an ever changing age.

For Phillips, three considerations need to
be given with regard to the changeless Christ in
the midst of a changing world.[35]

1. Jesus is still the center of faith.

2. His right to the spiritual leadership of
   mankind has remained unsurpassed through
   the centuries.

3. The fact of the incarnation is still true
   and applicable in human lives.

Phillips wondered,

How much of our modern sophistication comes
from our inability or unwillingness to distin-
guish between the variables and the constants
in human nature--the changes "out there" and
the unchanged realities within us.[36]

He tried to delineate the meaning of the phrase "Word of God," and came up with three specific meanings.[37] The "Word of God" includes the following:

1. The Word given--this is God's initiative in the lives of men.

2. The Word as definitive--this is the ultimate action of God in men's lives to the present time.

3. The Word is living--this is therefore not referring to the Bible, but to the dynamic action of God.

Paul Scherer has noted a similar dynamic quality of the living Word of God.

It lays hold of the stuff of human existence and reshapes it. It appropriates and transforms. It takes the things that are, and through them brings to birth the things that are not. It adopts the cultural pattern and by standing over against it fashions the new. It finds an old barrel-top, as Raphael did, and leaves it a Madonna of the Chair! It borrows of folk songs and writes a symphony. It takes the conflict that tears human life apart and speaks to them of wholeness and the strange peace of God. It takes the problems of guilt and death, of anxiety and despair, and speaks to them of a Kingdom. It takes man's estrangement from himself and from his fellows and from God, and talks of acceptance and belonging--which is the forgiveness of sin and justification by faith! This is precisely what the New Testament did, what the primitive Church did, and what needs to be done again.[38]

Samuel Miller drew a correlation between the Word and words.[39] He said that the preacher's great temptation is to multiply words at the expense of the Word.

Substitutions flow in from all sides; temptation rises from the very ground; custom
and tradition commend the easier way, and
ultimately the humble servant of the Word
becomes merely the pompous butler of mean-
ingless tid-bits. There is no silence left;
no sanctity, no reverberation of the earth
and sky, no shaking of the foundations as
when God speaks; there are simply talkative
men, garrulous, loose-tongued, lip-flapping
speel-masters, glib with God and giddy with
gab. None fall so low as those who presume
to speak the Word merely by mouthing words.[40]

Miller would not have the sermon merely be
a thespian but tawdry piece of verbiage. This
proclivity toward verbal counterfeiting by ministers led Miller to give the following invective.
"The church in America could stop preaching
tomorrow and the effect on human life and morals
would be measurable only if you had a very strong
magnifying glass to observe it."[41]

Miller drew upon Karl Barth's concept of the
Word of God and said: "Once the Word is heard,
then speech is born."[42] That the preacher himself first hears this Word before trying to convey
it to others is imperative.

His service for the Word will be known by his
workmanship with words. How far can he cut
down the distance between the Word and his
words? How can he achieve an intimacy, a
clarity, a transparency between them? How
well does he shape the words so they will
carry some echo of the great Word?[43]

When allowed to perform its true function, the
Word so operates as "to elicit the full reality
of man, in short, to open the way for his fulfill-
ment in the new being, for his life in the kingdom."[44]

H. Grady Davis said that the Word is the only
thing which can both communicate with us and
effect a change within us.[45]

The concept of God's word means that God is
sufficiently unlike us to have something to
say to us that only he can say, that we cannot say for ourselves or for him. It means
also that we are enough like him that he can
express his mind to us, and that he wishes
to do so.[46]

Preaching mediates the Word of God. The degree
of that mediation, said Davis, is the true mea-
sure of effective preaching.[47]

H. H. Farmer expressed a similar thought
regarding the Word of God as it comes through
the preacher and then the sermon.[48] Farmer insisted that "we cannot have right ideas on how
to preach unless we first have some right ideas
on what preaching essentially is and what it is
intended to effect."[49] The Word of God first
must make its way into our sermons, and then be
allowed to reach the hearers on its own terms.

Farmer had a warning regarding the dangers
of smothering the Word with words, that is, of
speaking words just because something must be
said rather than being possessed by the Word.

The deliberate and continuous seeking of
materials for preaching, if it be not excep-
tionally well disciplined and controlled, can
defeat its own end, and ultimately impoverish
the preacher's work rather than enrich it.
For it can both express and foster a narrow,
professional, second-hand attitude of mind,
which lacks the power to respond sensitively
and directly to the glory and wonder, the
humor and the tragedy, of human life itself.[50]

Thus, the Word of God must speak on its own
terms. It is this continuous speaking that vali-
dates ministry today as it was validated in the
first century. Regarding valid ministry,
T. W. Manson said: "What is the secret of its
staying-power? The answer of the whole New

51

Testament is that it is the Risen Christ himself
who is carrying it out."[51]

Judgment

William Muehl has said that another element
vital to the message is judgment.[52] The neglect
of this element has caused the Christian cause
great problems.

> The effort to define God's love in purely
> redemptive terms, to strip it of the ele-
> ment of judgment has given rise to the
> notion that anything goes if the people
> who are going love one another.[53]

The sense of the absence of evidence of God's
judgment in history is a result of what Muehl
called the "vulgarized Reformation," that is,
the telling of people that they are saved only
by grace and not works.[54] In the face of such
thought, the pulpit has five tasks regarding
judgment.[55]

1. The task of reaffirming the hard reality
   of God as judge rests upon the shoulders
   of the preacher.

2. Preachers must re-establish some significant relationships between human acts
   and the substance of divine justice.

3. People must be helped to see that God
   is not indifferent to what happens in
   creation.

4. Judgment must not be spoken of as "divine hostility."

5. The preacher must make a claim on behalf
   of the use of intelligence and imagination in perceiving God's judging will at
   work in life.

This very judgment has worked itself out
in history. Because of the "vulgar Reformation," people assumed that the reception of
divine grace leaves nothing else to be achieved
or hoped for in human existence. The ultimate
conclusion could well be this: "Once you have
Christ, you may as well drop dead!"[56] People
have been spoken to in terms of beginnings--
re-birth, re-newal, re-generation. But little
is said about the actual content of human life.
As Muehl asked, "We affirm Christ to be the
Alpha and the Omega. But what happens to the
rest of the alphabet?"[57] Judgment is therefore
not just part of the content of the sermon. It
is a reality which touches the preacher also
because of past failures.

G. Earl Guinn showed how this failure
occurred historically in ministry.[58] First,
"Expectancy gave way to complacency." This hap-
pened when the minister became a favored member
of society. Second, "The views of the ministry
supplanted the news of God." Creeds grew up as
replacements for personal faith and experience.
Ministers began to say, "Faith means what I say
it means." Third, "The ministry tried to serve
its interest through the power of government
rather than the power of God." It tried to
usher in the Kingdom via litigation. Fourth,
failure occurred by "allowing the cry of the
prophet to become the chant of the priest."

These four failures brought judgment upon
the Church in the process. Guinn pointed out
when preaching failed, the Church failed. Judgment is real.

Knowledge of Contemporary Events

The Gospel, the Word of God, and judgment
are all vital elements in the content of the
sermon. H. H. Farmer added another element.[59]
He said that the preacher must be aware of the
contemporary events around him, and that this

knowledge must find its way into sermons.

I plead for a preaching and teaching ministry which takes the trouble to acquire some
knowledge of the contemporary world of culture and is exercising a sound Christian
discrimination in regard to it; I plead for
a preaching and teaching ministry which,
without burking the very real difficulties
is nevertheless a powerful presentation of
the Christian absolutes and of their indis-
soluble connection with the whole Christian
view of God and man; I plead for a teaching
ministry which in relation to the frightful
problems of these times is challengingly and
trenchantly ethical and doctrinal at one and
the same time. Let our people, especially
our young people see the tremendous crisis
which confronts the world today, and the
cruciality of the part they are called to
play in it. Let them recover the sense
that whilst Christ does not call a man out
of the world, does call him to a decisive
break with the world, the sense that the
unconscious, acquiescence is unChristian
and half-Christian values in the ends we
pursue, the books we read, the political
judgments we make, is a most serious treach-
ery to God and to Christ and to mankind.
St. Paul's prayer for the Philippians comes
to mind again: the prayer that Christian men
in these chaotic days should be more and more
rich in knowledge and all manner of insight,
enabling them to have a sense of what is
vital.[60]

John Claypool concurred with this idea that
knowledge of what is happening in the lives of
people is crucial to the sermon.[61]

Pleading

The last element which is central to the
content of the sermon is a note of pleading for

a decision. This is not just a characteristic of the voice as a time of invitation, but a wooing throughout the sermon. John Mackay put it in the following terms:

> . . . there's one great function of Christian preaching, to preach for a real verdict, for a total response of personality, for repentence and faith, so that when the Gospel is proclaimed, this Christ who demands the total allegiance of human souls, as Saviour and Lord of life--what He wants is repentence . . . .
> . . . .
>
> . . . And preaching is successful, and only is successful when the people come to the point of being willing to say with John Calvin, "My heart I give the Lord, eagerly and sincerely." Then the Gospel becomes Good News in the inmost recesses of the heart and of mind.[62]

SOURCES OF THE MESSAGE

Some of the Mullins lecturers have dealt with the matter of the sources of the sermon. Their concerns involved God's revelation, the minister's experience with Christ, his own creativity, and the Bible.

Revelation

Paul Scherer reminded his hearers that they must always remember that the ultimate source of a sermon is God.[63] He said that the whole idea of God's revelation was not intended to lay out indisputable truths, but Himself.

> It (revelation) is not conceptual truth that God is intent on sharing. It is not first and foremost information He wants to impart. It is Himself, that not having seen Him we

may yet know Him and trust Him and live our
lives in Him, freely and for love's sake.[64]

God reveals himself through art, said
Samuel Miller.[65] Neither religion nor art is
concerned with surface appearances or with
superficial likenesses. Miller quoted sculptor
Henry Moore to convey his point: "Because a
work does not aim at reproducing natural appearances, it is not therefore an escape from life
but may be a penetration into reality."[66]
Miller also quoted Max Beckmann, the expression-
ist:

". . . all important things in art since Ur
of the Chaldees, since Tel Halaf and Crete, have
always originated in the deepest feeling about
the mystery of Being."[67] In this regard, Miller
had the following comments:

The genius of the artist is that he can see
so much in a loaf of bread and a glass of
wine on the table, or in a clown grotesquely
painted, looking into the distance, or in
the wrinkled face of an old woman; or in
old houses cluttered on a hillside; or in a
kitchen chair marked and worn; or at a woman
looking at her firstborn child. The genius
of a minister--is it any different? Is he
not to see grace in the common things, unex-
pected mercy in routine, the kingdom of
heaven within the heart of ordinary man,
the beauty of the Lord in the habitations
of men, the hallelujah of the heart in the
plain home-spun lives, the sight of angels
in sordid places? What is the minister but
one gifted and trained to see in life what
others may miss?[63]

This statement says much about the minister himself, but it also speaks of the revelatory
nature of the mundane in life as being the source
of the sermon.

Deep Experience With Christ

Another source of the sermon is the preacher's own deep Christian experience. This experience moves the preacher into a risk taking position, because the experience must first possess and transform him. Joseph Sittler spoke of this matter in the following terms:

> To be a preacher is not only to know eschatology as a report and an agenda item in systematic theology; he is, in the anguish of his task, the eschatological man. The work of his mind is the intellectual form of his obedience. The preacher by burden of his office can have no authentic selfhood if he repudiates this way, or by acceptable forms of betrayal, seeks another. Other ways there are, to be sure, and the prestige and piety of them may mask for a lifetime the fact of betrayal. The institution and the world want adjustment, not anguish. And one may even understand his theological education as tutelage toward acquiescence in non-anguish.[69]

Sittler quoted two significant statements from Luther on this matter. "I did not learn my theology all at once, but I had to search deeper for it, where my temptations took me."[70] "A man becomes a theologian by living, by dying, and by being damned, not by understanding, reading, and speculation." All of this says that the minister struggles in his experience with Christ, but that every struggle becomes the source of making the gospel meaningful to others. Sittler said that without this experiential element, the gospel is simply ignored by men. Unless the preacher himself is affected by an experience with Christ, he cannot live or communicate the gospel "with a bigness appropriate to the public, materially-related, operationally-actualized character of his living days."[71]

57

This experiential element is also the reason that, in a sense, preaching cannot be taught. Sittler put it this way:

Disciplines correlative to preaching can be taught, but preaching as an act of witness cannot be taught. Biblical introduction, training in languages, methods of exegesis, culture, and other historical data that illuminate the texts of the Scriptures--these matters can be refined and transmitted in teaching. But preaching itself, the creative symbiosis within which intersects numberless facts, experience, insights, felt duties of pastoral obligation toward a specific congregation, the interior existence of the preacher himself, this particular man as he seeks for right utterance of an uncommunicable and non-sharable quality of being and thought--this cannot be taught.[72]

Thus, the Christian experience of the preacher himself is a source of the sermon.

Creativity

The creative process within the preacher is another source of the sermon. H. Grady Davis has said that this process is a sine qua non.[73] He explicated his idea as follows:

A genuine sermon is more like something done to the preacher than like something he does, and it begins in a moment of hearing the word as if he had never heard it before, in a moment of vision, of seeing freshly, as if his eyes had suddenly been opened for the first time.[74]

Davis went on to say that, as with scientists, the preacher will have sermons which seem to "come to him." This is his own imagination and creativity at work.

This is the way your very best sermons will
come. It will not come out of your own
intense desire and sustained effort to hear,
to see. It will not come without the thought
and intelligent and concentrated study that
represents your own best attempts. But when
it comes, it will come in an act of recognition, and afterwards you can only say, "It
came to me."[75]

Finally, Davis summed up his thoughts on the
matter of creativity this way:

For preaching is not telling, but being
told. It is not a word going out from a
man, but a word coming to a man and through
him. It is not giving something, but shar-
ing something that is given. It begins not
in knowledge, but in vision, a kind of "in-
ward beholding," as Samuel Taylor Coleridge
called it. A true sermon is not a fabrica-
tion, but a discovery. It is not a creation,
but on man's part a recognition, and on God's
part a revelation.[76]

The Bible

    One surprise to this researcher was that
while several lecturers mentioned the Bible as
being a source for the sermon, few of them
expatiated on the matter. Salutary credits were
accorded the Bible, but little substance was
devoted to it.

    Exceptions do exist, however, although the
references are relatively minor. H. Grady Davis
said that the Bible is the standard of judgment
by which to test the scattered imaginations of
our proud hearts.[77] We must hear the Bible
"because the Bible is given by him who gives all
good things. It is not only a message from
heaven; it is also a messenger in the biblical
sense, an aggelos, an angel."[78]

59

John Claypool said that listening to the
Bible is the only way by which he can preach
with integrity.[79] George Buttrick said that
the Gospel is mediated through the Scriptures,
and the preacher is therefore obligated to be
faithful to the Bible.[80]

Again, it must be pointed out that this
theme simply was not treated at length by the
lecturers. The pervasive mood indicates that
they want the preacher to be a biblical aficio-
nado. In all, this matter was taken for
granted.

STYLE

The matter of style was a topic in Horton
Davies' 1961 Mullins lectures.[81] Looking at the
Victorian pulpit, Davies concluded that style
was an extremely important element in sermons of
that era. For one thing, to the nineteenth century English audience, "sermon-tasting was both
a duty and a delight."[82] The people loved vari-
ety and great oratory, and styles developed to
meet those tastes. Styles ran the gamut--the
thespian, the effusive, the tawdry, the prolix
and desultory comments, the vituperative style,
and even the conversational style. In fact,
Thomas Binney is said to have begun a pulpit
revolution with his conversational preaching,
described as "inspired talk."[83]

In general, the Victorian sermons were
characterized by the following elements of
style: topical sermons with specious text selec-
tion; frequent and unashamed appeal to emotions,
especially fear and pity; the use of wit and
humor; and a delight in scenic grandeur, utiliz-
ing scenes from nature and the works of the
Romantic poets.[84] Moreover, sermons of that
era could incarnate ideas. For example, John
Henry Newman was able to "invest abstract and
complex philosophical theology with movement
and life," and to make the "realities of the

invisible world seem so vivid that the material
world seemed a mere shadow."[85]

The preacher of today cannot merely mimic
the style of the Victorian pulpit. As G. Earl
Guinn has shown, such mimetic action is totally
unnecessary.[86] He asked what kind of preaching
people listen to today. It is that preaching
which "simply and honestly tries to help people
understand themselves, their fellows, and their
times in light of the knowledge of God."[87] John
Claypool concurred, saying in one lecture that
the preacher's style must be in keeping with his
personality.[88]

Style has much to do with even the choice
of words in the sermon. John Mackay said this
as follows:

> We have got to analyze every phrase and word
> we use, to see that we get the most out of
> words; and in many instances we have got to
> use new words that have never been used in
> preaching before, and in sermons which
> people understand and which stab them and
> shock them.[89]

Mackay said that good examples of this kind of
style are found in the writings of people like
C.S. Lewis and Dorothy Sayers.

Joseph Sittler quoted Dan O. Via, Jr. when
he spoke to this issue:

> What kind of language best represents and
> communicates the event of Jesus of Nazareth,
> the Christ, and does most justice to the
> affirmation . . . that God has disclosed
> Himself in human life?"[90]

The preacher's task is to answer this question
and form his style around that answer.

DELIVERY

The delivery of the sermon is an important,
but often ignored, factor in preaching. Yet, as
Theodore Adams said, a pastor may be good at many
things, but if he cannot preach, he will never get
a chance to do any of them.[91] Adams' comment
includes content but emphasizes the oral delivery
of the sermon in an acceptable fashion.

William Muehl recounted an incident in which
he spoke in a church without using a manuscript.[92]
The reception was quite favorable. It seemed that
the use of a manuscript in delivering a sermon
erects a barrier between the preacher and congregation. Said Muehl, "The most powerfully written,
the most eloquently delivered of manuscript sermons has an uphill struggle in the minds of a great
many people . . . ."[93]

On the other hand, manuscript-free delivery
does not guarantee success, especially if the
preacher is not careful to prepare and give the
sermon in orderly fashion. Desultory delivery is
deadly. Harold Cooke Phillips put it like this:

> . . . some sermons are like swamps--they
> oose [sic] out all over the place. Others
> are like rivers--the difference between a
> swamp and a river is that the river has
> banks. These give direction and movement.
> Some sermons are like the world before the
> Eternal intervened--they are without form
> and void and darkness is upon the face of
> the congregation![94]

George Buttrick also used the river meta-
phor when speaking of delivering a sermon:

> Let the sermon flow like a river, with here
> a stretch of rapids and there a quiet pool,
> with bridges to punctuate the journey, with
> views to stir the traveller, with no sunken
> logs or capsized boats, and at the end some
> city of God.[95]

Buttrick further emphasized the fact that the preacher must be natural in his voice and stance while delivering the sermon.

SETTING

For the most part, the setting for the sermon will be the worship service. While sermons are given at other occasions, the worship experience is the setting for the majority of sermons.

H. H. Farmer gave an entire lecture on this subject.[96] He framed his argument as follows:

> Preaching needs worship, the setting of worship in order to keep the personality of the preacher in its proper place and proportion. The preacher needs the protection of worship against certain obvious dangers to his soul. But the congregation needs its protection against the preacher, if I may so put it. It needs its protection against his weakness, if he is weak. For him the weakness of his utterance is plainly of less account, if it be but a small part of a great act of worship wherein men are lifted in adoration and thanksgiving, in confession and intercession, into the very presence of God. But it needs its protection also against his strength, if he be strong, if he be what is known as a powerful and popular preacher whom crowds flock to hear.[97]

At the same time, worship needs preaching so that worship will be personal enough. Preaching done in such a context can satisfy three fundamental human needs, said Farmer. These include:

1. The need for release from the finite, or the need for an adequate end.[98]

2. The need for release from the instinctive,
    or the need for a right attitude.

3. The need for release from the ego, or the
    proper humility.

Christian preaching gets its "otherworld-
ly" elements from worship. This "otherworldli-
ness" says that the true meaning of our life "is
not to be found in this world considered in and
for itself, but rather in what this world is
leading on to in 'the beyond' of this world."[99]
For this reason, said Farmer, every sermon "must
be informed with the spirit of worship."[100]
Farmer said:

> We must ask ourselves this question con-
> cerning every sermon we prepare: does it
> so plainly set forth, (or if it does not
> set it forth in plain statement, is it so
> deeply penetrated and infused by) the
> vision of God's holy claim upon us in
> Christ, that men must surely feel again
> its condemnation and its call penetrating
> again their own soul.[101]

Horton Davies noted the dangers of an
imbalance between preaching and worship with
regard to the Victorian pulpit.[102] He said that
popular preaching often became a substitute for
worship. "The greater the preacher's popular
appeal, the greater the danger."[103] This danger
did not end in the nineteenth century. Today's
preachers need to give heed to Farmer's warning
above.

One of Donald Macleod's lectures was
entitled, "Theology Gives Meaning and Shape to
Worship."[104] He said that Christian worship is
different from other types of worship for three
reasons:

1. Its presuppositions are different.

2. The Christian's involvement in it is different.

3. The Christian's intention with regard to it is different.

This difference shapes the preacher's message. If it does not, liturgical anarchy arises. Macleod gave two reasons for this anarchy.[105] First, the act of worship is not a product of theological meanings. Second, the worshipping congregation "has not captured from the shape of the service a vision of life's ideal pattern and, therefore, they do not emerge from the church as a reconciling force in the world."[106]

Preaching and worship exist in a symbiotic relationship. Worship is more than just the context for the sermon. It gives content, background, and theological support. James McCord described preaching as a "representative ministry."[107] It is not a solo performance, but a task done within the worship setting.

FORM

Substance precedes form in the sermon, but once the substance is garnered, the element of form must be considered. Two of the Mullins lecturers have dealt with this matter. They are Joseph Sittler and Kelley Miller Smith.

Sittler set the tone of his argument as follows:

As we confront the problem of faith and form we must be blasted out of our common assumptions that we can solve the problem by technique, fresh materials, or drown out chaos by raising our voices, find some happy trick with the look of modernity about it . . . .[108]

65

Sittler said that three things are needed if
faith is to take up new forms which will serve
it today. First, what is needed is doctrinal
clarification concerning the church, the word,
the sacraments "as shall restore to them their
holy, particular, biblically attested source,
power and meaning."109 The "Word" is Christ
himself as the concretion in redemptive action
of the love of God, "and if the preacher of the
word be not thus centered, it cannot avoid
being swallowed up by categories of moral counsel and religious idealism."110

Second, we must seek a form of the church
that announces faith in these realities--
and then trust the power and integrity of
those realities to accomplish their own
work of beauty, grace, and evocation.
Beauty is a product of truth; it is not
a cosmetic.
Third, we must, I believe, perform a
resolute calculated act of purgation.
The church building as such is a symbol;
it is not simply a place to hand symbols.
If indeed it be in its total form a single
symbol, there can be an antiseptic reduc-
tion in the nature and number of symbols
within. We must purge out the cluttered
and cluttering accumulation of secondary
"church" effects, the thoughtless conven-
tions, the mild cliches, the automatic
repetitions, the taken-for-granted. The
huge and growing categories of church
"symbols" must be subjected to purgation.
And out of symbolic poverty we may again
be open to new and intelligible beckon-
ings.111

Kelley Miller Smith has said that form is
intrinsically bound up with substance.112 The
preacher does not have the choice between having
form and structure or not having it. His choice
is between having thought out orderly structure,
or one that is not thought out and is possibly
chaotic.

The chances of effectiveness in the presentation of an urgent message which addresses
social crises are greatly reduced when no
thought is given to the manner of presentation and when the preacher does not have the
natural gifts to embark upon an effective
form without deliberate effort.[113]

Smith further noted that the real task of the
preacher is to find the form which already
belongs to the idea, and make it as effective
as possible. There is form implicit in the idea
which is held.

CRAFTSMANSHIP[114]

Craftsmanship refers to the fashioning of
the various segments and components of a sermon
into a complete whole. The importance of craftsmanship was discussed by George Buttrick who
said that even the Good News of God could be
spoiled by bad craftsmanship.[115] The preacher,
as craftsman, is both "artist and day-laborer."[116]
He must know his task, his resources, his objectives, and he must work.

The preacher needs to select a text with
great care.[117] Next, he must "write down his
intention under God for that sermon"[118] His
thought for that text should be written down,
that is, he must answer the question, "Why did
this text attract me?" The text should be exe-
geted, and a new outline prepared. The introduction should be brief, succinct, and controlled.
The body of the sermon should "move steadily
toward its mark."[119]

The body is to display imagination in
development, as "sermon methods are almost
legion."[120] They include the expository, the
topical, the story, and the method which "sing-
les out from a Bible story certain salient
features, and weaves them into a sermon."[121]

67

The sermon is to have momentum, moving in a stair-step ascending fashion. The conclusion should be brief and should plead for a verdict. It should send the people home remembering, not the preacher, but Christ.

Buttrick insisted that the sermon be written out in full so that "it may be wrought with clarity, its diction into penetration, its style into persuasive truth."[122] It need not be read from the manuscript, however. Of diction, Buttrick said, "Noble and arresting diction consists, not in unusual words . . . but in the unusual linking of usual words."[123]

John Claypool discussed his own craftsmanship in his 1974 lectures. He outlined the process in four major divisions.[124]

1. How do I find something to preach about?

   A. Listen to self, to see what I need.
   B. Listen to the times and what people are thinking.
   C. Listen to what is happening in people's lives.

2. How do I formulate a sermon in response to what I have heard?

   A. Listen for the Scriptures to speak to those needs.
   B. Ask some laymen to help shape the sermon.

3. How can I finally shape the sermon? Claypool admitted that this is the hardest part, but that he writes and rewrites it.

4. What do I do after the sermon has been delivered? He has dialogue with laymen and ask them, "What did you hear?"

Robert J. McCracken devoted three lectures
to craftsmanship.[125] He said that the preacher
should "set himself to traverse the entire
ground of Christian truth, and to do so system-
atically, periodically, and as comprehensively
as he knows how."[126] How is the preacher to do
this? "We can secure the comprehensive coverage,
especially necessary in the case of an extended
ministry, if we make a practice of following a
clearly devised pattern in sermon construc-
tion."[127] One way to do so is to vary the
approach of the sermon along the divisions of
classical homiletics, namely, expository, ethical, devotional, theological, apologetical,
social, psychological, and evangelistic preaching.

Of expository preaching, McCracken said
that frequent biblical exposition keeps the
preacher from indulging his own predilections
and gives to him a limitless source of material.
There are some problems, however.

It cannot be overemphasized that the
primary consideration in biblical exposition is to maintain interest and keep
close to life. The weakness of much
expository preaching is twofold; it
inclines to be tedious and colorless,
and it is often detached and remote
from the activities and concerns of
everyday existence.[128]

Ethical preaching is not merely building
"moralisms" into sermons. It is, instead,
preaching founded on the knowledge of God's
grace and his demands. Devotional preaching
is the preaching of sermons whose design is
the deepening of the spiritual life. American preaching is weakest in the area of theological preaching, said McCracken, but it needs
to be strong.[129]

Theological preaching is an absolute neces-
sity. As rational beings we are under obligation
to reflect on our experience and to seek to
understand it. By itself, the practical side of
religion cannot finally satisfy us; we must have
an interpretation of it.[130]

Apologetic preaching combines both the
kerygma and the didache. Social sermons deal
with both causes and cures of social problems.

By and large the American pulpit is much too
prone to accept the political and economic
limitations which secularizing influences
would impose, among them the dictum that
whatever is economically right cannot be
morally wrong. It suffers the world to
draw boundaries all around the Christian
religion and for the most part has been
content to retire and remain within those
boundaries.[131]

. . . .

. . . it is the business of the preacher
to propound Christian principles and to
point out where the existing social order
is at variance with them. His task is to
stimulate the social conscience by working
out the implications of the Gospel in
national and international life.[132]

In this regard, McCracken reminded the preacher
that he is certain to "find himself at odds with
anything which is contrary to the good purpose
of God."[133]

The craft of building psychological sermons
involves allowing fundamental concepts of psychological insight to come to bear upon specific
issues. In evangelistic preaching, the preacher
structures his material in order to call for a
verdict.

SUMMARY

This chapter has dealt with the message,
the sermon. The lecturers said that Gospel is
the heart of the sermon and is itself the impe-
tus for preaching. The Word of God is the
dynamic force within the sermon. Insight into
contemporary events pervades the sermon. Finally,
the element of pleading is a vital aspect of the
content of the sermon.

The sources of the sermon are found in the
revelation of God of himself, the preacher's own
deep experience with Christ, in his creativity,
and the Bible. The style of the sermon has to do
with its wording and phrasing, and is an expres-
sion of the preacher's individuality. Styles of
other eras cannot be followed effectively today.

The delivery of the sermon seems best done
without the aid of a manuscript or of notes. The
preacher's entire mien affects delivery. The setting of the sermon is primarily the service of
worship. The sermon and worship exist in a symbiotic relationship, benefiting each other as only
each can.

The form of the sermon is important in
determining the effectiveness of a given sermon.
Form is fundamental to content. Craftsmanship
refers to the preacher's ability to fashion the
materials of his message into one harmonious
unit. All components of the sermon play an
important role in regard to the preacher's craftsmanship.

FOOTNOTES

[1]George A. Buttrick, "What Is The Gospel?" (Louisville: Boyce Library, The Southern Baptist Theological Seminary, 1943), p. 1. (Mimeographed.)

[2]Ibid.

[3]Ibid., p. 17.

[4]H. Grady Davis, "The Contemporary World" (Louisville: Boyce Library, The Southern Baptist Theological Seminary, 1962), p. 23. (Mimeographed.)

[5]Paul Scherer, "Preaching As A Radical Transaction" (Louisville: Boyce Library, The Southern Baptist Theological Seminary, 1957), p. 1. (Mimeographed.)

[6]Ibid., pp. 3-19.

[7]Ibid., p. 1.

[8]Ibid., p. 19.

[9]Ibid., p. 28.

[10]Ibid., p. 29.

[11]Ibid., pp. 30-1.

[12]Ibid., p. 33.

[13]Ibid., pp. 33-4.

[14]Ibid., p. 37.

[15]Paul Scherer, "The Credibility and Relevance of the Gospel" (Louisville: Boyce Library, The Southern Baptist Theological Seminary, 1957). (Mimeographed.)

[16]Ibid., p. 5.

[17]Ibid., p. 9.

[18]Ibid., p. 13.

[19]Ibid., p. 16.

[20]Ibid., p. 19.

[21]Ibid., p. 19.

[22]Ibid., p. 21.

[23]Ibid., p. 30.

[24]Ibid., p. 28.

[25]William Muehl, "A Sense of Loss" (Louisville: Boyce Library, The Southern Baptist Theological Seminary, 1975), p. 4. (Mimeographed.)

[26]Ibid.

[27]Ibid., p. 5.

[28]Ibid., p. 7.

[29]Ibid., p. 10.

[30]Ibid.

[31]Ibid., p. 16.

[32]Ibid., pp. 20-21.

[33]Ibid., p. 22.

[34]Harold Cooke Phillips, "The Eternal Word" (Louisville: Boyce Library, The Southern Baptist Theological Seminary, 1964), pp. 1-2 (Mimeographed.)

[35]Ibid., pp. 2-3.

[36]Ibid., p. 3.

[37]Harold Cooke Phillips, "The Word of God" (Louisville: Boyce Library, The Southern Baptist Theological Seminary, 1964), pp. 1-5. (Mimeographed.)

[38]Scherer, "The Credibility and Relevance of the Gospel," p. 27.

[39]Samuel H. Miller, "The Word of God--and Words" (Louisville: Boyce Library, The Southern Baptist Theological Seminary, 1963), pp. 1-2. (Mimeographed.)

[40]Ibid., p. 2.

[41]Ibid., p. 3.

[42]Ibid., p. 7.

[43]Ibid., p. 9.

[44]Ibid., p. 18.

[45]H. Grady Davis, "The Personal Word" (Louisville: Boyce Library, The Southern Baptist Theological Seminary, 1962), p. 3. (Mimeographed.)

[46]Ibid.

[47]Ibid., p. 4.

[48]H. H. Farmer, "Preaching and Worship," Review and Expositor, XLIII, No. 3 (1946), pp. 244ff.

[49]Ibid., p. 244.

[50]Ibid., p. 245.

[51]T.W. Manson, The Servant-Messiah (Grand Rapids: Baker Book House, 1977 reprint), p. 98.

[52]William Muehl, "The Depth of Judgment" (Louisville: Boyce Library, The Southern Baptist Theological Seminary, 1975), p. 12. (Mimeographed.)

[53]Ibid.

[54]Ibid., p. 16.

[55]Ibid., pp. 18-20.

[56]Muehl, "The Breadth of Compassion," p. 3.

[57]Ibid., p. 13.

[58]G. Earl Guinn, in a lecture ("That the Ministry Might Not Be Ashamed") at The Southern Baptist Theological Seminary, March, 1960 (tape recording on file at Boyce Library).

[59]H. H. Farmer, "The Preacher and Culture," Review and Expositor, XLIV, No. 1 (1947), pp. 35-49.

[60]Ibid., p. 49.

[61]John Claypool, in a lecture ("Listening and Preaching") at the Southern Baptist Theological Seminary, March, 1974 (on file at Boyce Library).

[62]John MacKay, "The Cosmic Christ" (Louisville: Boyce Library, The Southern Baptist Theological Seminary, 1948), pp. 45-46. (Mimeographed.)

[63]Paul Scherer, "The Nature of Revelation" (Louisville: Boyce Library, The Southern Baptist Theological Seminary, 1957), p. 8. (Mimeographed.)

[64]Ibid.

[65]Samuel Miller, "The Vision of Reality--And Art" (Louisville: Boyce Library, The Southern Baptist Theological Seminary, 1963), p. 6. (Mimeographed.)

[66] Ibid.

[67] Ibid.

[68] Ibid., p. 9.

[69] Sittler, The Anguish of Preaching, pp. 32-3.

[70] Ibid., p. 33.

[71] Ibid., p. 37.

[72] Ibid., pp. 12-13.

[73] H. Grady Davis, "The Moment of Recognition" (Louisville: Boyce Library, The Southern Baptist Theological Seminary, 1962), p. 39. (Mimeographed).

[74] Ibid., p. 38.

[75] Ibid., p. 40.

[76] Ibid., p. 46.

[77] H. Grady Davis, "The Personal Word" (Louisville: Boyce Library, The Southern Theological Seminary, 1962), p. 11. (Mimeographed.)

[78] Ibid.

[79] John Claypool, in a lecture ("Listening and Preaching") at The Southern Baptist Theological Seminary, March, 1974 (tape on file at Boyce Library).

[80] George Buttrick, "What Is The Gospel?" (Louisville: Boyce Library, The Southern Baptist Theological Seminary, 1944), pp. 17-20. (Mimeographed.)

[81] Horton Davies, "The Power of the Victorian Pulpit," Worship and Theology in England: From

Newman to Martineau, 1850-1900, "Worship and
Theology in England," Vol. 4 (Princeton:
Princeton University Press, 1962), pp. 283-
348.

[82]Ibid., p. 283.

[83]Ibid., p. 287.

[84]Ibid., pp. 287-298.

[85]Ibid., p. 308.

[86]G. Earl Guinn, in a lecture ("That the
Ministry Might Not Be Ashamed") at The Southern
Baptist Theological Seminary, March, 1960 (tape
on file at Boyce Library).

[87]Ibid.

[88]Claypool, "Listening and Preaching."

[89]Mackay, "The Cosmic Christ."

[90]Joseph Sittler, quoting Don O. Via, Jr.,
The Anguish of Preaching, p. 19.

[91]Theodore Adams, "The Preacher Looks at
Himself and His People" (Louisville: The
Southern Baptist Theological Seminary, 1956),
p. 2. (Mimeographed.)

[92]William Muehl, "A Sense of Loss," pp. 1-2.

[93]Ibid., pp. 2-3.

[94]Harold Cooke Phillips, "Communicating the
Word of God," p. 1.

[95]George Buttrick, "The Craftsmanship of
the Preacher (B)," p. 17.

[96]H. H. Farmer, "Preaching and Worship,"
pp. 243-260.

[97] Ibid., p. 246.

[98] Ibid., p. 250.

[99] Ibid., p. 254.

[100] Ibid., p. 255.

[101] Ibid., p. 258.

[102] Horton Davies, "The Power of the Victorian Pulpit," p. 346.

[103] Ibid.

[104] Donald Macleod, in a lecture, ("Theology Gives Meaning and Shape to Worship") at The Southern Baptist Theological Seminary, March, 1970 (tape recording on file at Boyce Library).

[105] Ibid., p. 4_.

[106] Ibid.

[107] James McCord, in a Lecture (unnamed, but fourth in a series), at The Southern Baptist Theological Seminary, March, 1977 (tape recording on file at Boyce Library).

[108] Joseph Sittler, The Anguish of Preaching, p. 54.

[109] Ibid., p. 64.

[110] Ibid., p. 63.

[111] Ibid.

[112] Kelley Miller Smith, in a Lecture ("The Relevance of Structure") at The Southern Baptist Theological Seminary, March, 1971 (tape recording on file at Boyce Library).

[113] Ibid.

[114]Craftsmanship has to do with what the preacher does, and could easily fit into Chapter II. Since the actual fitting together of the pieces is the focus, however, this item was reserved for this chapter.

[115]George Buttrick, "Power--And The Man," p. 15.

[116]George Buttrick, "The Craftsmanship of the Preacher (A)," p. 1.

[117]Ibid., pp. 3-22.

[118]Ibid., p. 6.

[119]Ibid., p. 10.

[120]Ibid., p. 12.

[121]Ibid., p. 15.

[122]Ibid., p. 19.

[123]Ibid., p. 20.

[124]John Claypool, in a lecture, ("Listening and Preaching") at The Southern Baptist Theological Seminary, March, 1974 (tape recording on file at Boyce Library).

[125]Robert J. McCracken, The Making of the Sermon (New York: Harper and Brothers, 1956), chapters 2, 3, and 4.

[126]Ibid., p. 24.

[127]Ibid., p. 26.

[128]Ibid., p. 36.

[129]Ibid., p. 43.

[130]Ibid., p. 47.

[131]Ibid., pp. 51-52.

[132]Ibid., pp. 53-54.

[133]Ibid., p. 54.

CHAPTER IV

THE AUDIENCE

The third element in Aristotle's triad is the audience. Aristotle felt that the speaker needes to know his audience as well as possible, and that such knowledge is the key to effective communication. In the realm of homiletics, the audience is primarily the congregation, the people to whom the speaker (preacher) brings an orally delivered message (sermon).

IMPORTANCE OF THE AUDIENCE

"Individualism is a curse of American church life," said Roger Fredrikson.[1] This individualism can expose, in a negative way, the importance of the audience. Fredrikson said that the churches which are making an impact are those which have great congregational life. Such good congregational life is not easily attained, however, It is something on which the minister must constantly work, and this work can be fostered only by a genuine love. Samuel Miller said that as ministers, "Our basic service, if we love the Lord, is the care of souls."[2] He spoke of this care in connection with the minister's work of building fellowship within the congregation. Miller emphasized the uniqueness and potential of persons who comprise any church.

There is more wealth of human mystery and miracle in any six people taken at random for our congregations than we as ministers can care for and illumine in a whole lifetime of service.[3]

This discussion thus far has emphasized the importance of the minister within the congregation, but the congregation itself has a life apart from the minister, and has its own intrinsic value. This value can be positive

81

or negative. Theodore Adams said, "Preaching
is foolishness . . . unless it is backed by the
lives of the believers. Your congregation can
cancel out much of what you say by their
lives."[4] [italics not in the original.]

H. Grady Davis had a similar emphasis,
and said that the collective witness of the
congregation is important.[5] The preacher cannot be treated as an isolated "pulpit prima
donna." Davis' comments which follow explain
his views:

> That theory of preaching centered almost
> exclusively in the man in the pulpit, the
> individual preacher, as man, as scholar
> and teacher, as believer, as man of per-
> sonal charm and power, as prophet and man
> of vision, and so on. It looked at him
> ideally, saw him as a paragon, a hero
> fighting the Lord's battle single-
> handedly. It saw him as a religious
> viruoso, who had overcome all difficul-
> ties and solved all problems, and could
> from his wealth of wisdom and experience
> meet the needs of those who heard him.
> He was like a Moses to the people around
> him.[6]

Two great problems exist with such a view, said
Davis. "First, it practically ignores the church,
the Christian community which produced the preacher, from within which only can he speak."[7] Second,
it ignores the transcendental elements. "If we
are to hear the personal word of God at all, we
must hear it through the church."[8] [italics not
in the original.] Thus, the word which the
minister preaches is the word of the entire
Christian community. This fact underscores the
extreme value of the congregation in the trans-
mission of the Word of God. As Davis put it,
"without the voice of the church we have no
dependable assurance that what we think we hear
is indeed the word."[9]

Davis also said, "Together we are something no one of us is or can be apart."[10]

> From first to last, the whole New Testament's picture of our Christian existence is the picture of a corporate existence, not an existence as independent individuals. It is the picture of an existence in which no person can be a Christian in himself alone. No man can be in vital union with Christ without being in vital union with all other persons who are in union with Christ.[11]

This union is more than merely conviviality or gregarious behavior. It is a union welded by the spirit of the living Christ.

George Buttrick has said that in reality the act of preaching can occur only within the corporate milieu.[12] "Preaching is not divorced from the Church. The congregation also helps to shape the sermon, and to determine its power."[13] "Preaching is not divorced from corporate prayer of a faithful Church."[15]

The attitude of the congregation has a direct bearing upon the work of the church as a whole, and on the minister in particular. The counsel of William Muehl was directed at this fact:

> I am sure that a considerable part of the fatigue which often haunts us when we sit down to compose the word in a given week . . . arises from an often unidentified feeling that the homiletical task is really not very important. The tendency toward oversimplification . . . arises from the congregation's insistence that complexity and faith are at opposite ends of some spiritual spectrum, --from the unwillingness of Protestant lay men and women to use the resources of their minds to receive and apply the gospel.[16]

This whole attitude, said Muehl, is built upon a lie, which is the "insistence upon quick and easy answers to the massive complexity of our relationship with God."[17]

John Claypool pointed out the fact that the preacher must move people into accepting their roles as lay ministers, thereby fulfilling the demands of the gospel.[18] This emphasis served to stress further the importance of the congregation.

ANALYSIS OF THE AUDIENCE

Who are the people in the audience? What are they like? What do they think? These questions, and others, confront anyone who tries to come to grips with the makeup of a given audience. Some of the Mullins lecturers have dealt with just such questions, trying to tell their hearers to know how to communicate better with their congregations.

John Mackay said that people in the churches are recipients of some of the same wounds which inflict society at large.[19] These wounds include "the existence of a great void, an abysmal emptiness, an eerie vacuum."[20] People are marked by a feeling of anonymity, finality, and loneliness. These men and women with these specific maladies need a true, clear, and powerful word from God. Preachers have a responsibility to know those needs of the people and speak directly to them. John Mackay spoke of this process of communicating the word of God directly to a congregation.

. . . the more real we can be about the human situation in its contemporary, historical and cosmic aspects, the more powerfully and luminously shall we be able to proclaim the Gospel, and with more relevance to the problems of real men and women in their life and in their thought. In other words, the Gospel of God is not going to be something

superstitious, or romantic, or mystical,
or unrelated to life. It is the thing that
is most related to life and to actual
thought.[21]

Yet, this attempt to know thoroughly the
audience in order to speak directly to it is
extraordinarily difficult. The communication
may not proceed well. Paul Scherer told what
happens when such is the case.

The young preacher finds pretty soon that
he isn't on speaking terms with his people.
Nobody knows what he is talking about. So
he becomes discouraged, and after a while
chucks the whole thing, to fall back on the
old hodge-podge and gobblydegook, [sic]
with a few positive thought about negative
reactions, and a little advice on the
subject of God's will for the brotherhood--
which, by the way, was the substance of the
devil's first sermon in the garden of Eden![22]

Scherer noted that the people to whom ministers
speak are children of the Enlightenment and the
Renaissance. They seem to say regarding religion, "Give us facts and evidences."[23] To such
people, religious language "can scarcely be
called language: it's gibberish. It comes from
Mars. It's the final reductio ad absurdum."[24]

Donald Macleod said that persons who comprise today's congregation possess four distinct
characteristics.[25]

1. People have a picture-conscious mentality.
    The media have shaped this mind-set.

2. People are shaped by a "hit psychology."
    This is a carryover from the realm of
    entertainment. It says that this event,
    even a worship event, must be "better"
    and "more exciting" than the preceding
    one, and the next is to be more spec-
    tacular than this one.

85

3. People possess the composite characters of art and science. These emphasize creativity and imagination, along with emotion. Usual Christian worship, however, is cerebral, one-sided, and non-awefulled.

4. People have contemporary symbols which communicate with them. The preacher must know what these symbols are, and which ones do not communicate to them.

John Claypool also spoke of knowing which symbols are appropriate.[26] Moreover, he noted that the mass media mind-set which people have requires preachers to be "entrepreneurs of a corporate worship experience. We are going to have to learn to be liturgists."[27] Liturgy will help preachers find the symbols which communicate.

APPROACH TO THE AUDIENCE

Assuming that the preacher knows his audience, the question arises concerning his approach to the audience as a collective body. How does the preacher reach his congregation?

Rapport

H.H. Farmer dealt extensively with the matter of rapport.[28] He began by saying that true preaching is intensely personal and that fact itself establishes a personal rapport between speaker and hearer. The preacher must "establish such a personal relationship with them that each feels . . . that you are speaking to him personally."[29] How does this happen? "I believe very strongly that our power to establish a personal relationship with man through preaching will vary with the extent to which we are learning to _love_ them . . . ."[30] Putting the matter succinctly, Farmer said:

86

. . . all effective preaching has an
indefinable note of winsomeness in it.
Winsomeness, as distinct from merely
hypnotic power, is precisely the capacity
at one in the same time to individualize
and to draw.[31]

To love people in preaching does not indi-
cate that the preacher needs to be weak. Farmer
had three comments regarding this subject.

1. You only really love a person when you
   see him in some degree as an absolutely
   unique individual who is not like anybody else. Preachers often develop a
   narrow "professional interest" in people,
   as souls to be saved.[32]

2. You have sympathy for people. This is a
   specifically Christian sympathy. It is
   the power to penetrate objectively yet
   feelingly (not emotionally) into the
   individual self-awareness of any man
   with whom we have to deal. Such em-
   pathy will give that strong winsomeness of mature love to preaching without which it will lack real effectiveness.[34]

3. We love others by relating to them as
   thinking persons. Preaching is therefore teaching, also. In these ways
   rapport is established with a congregation.

SUMMARY

Little was actually said about the congregation, especially when compared with the amount
of material on the speaker and the message. What
was said emphasized the fact that the audience
has a share in the effectiveness, or lack of it,
of the Gospel. Persons exist in relation to
other Christians.

The thinking of the people in the congregations today is shaped by mass media. The preacher must know how to speak to such a mindset. To do so requires that the preacher love his people and establish a good rapport with them.

FOOTNOTES

[1]Roger Fredrikson, in a lecture ("The Meaning of Christian Community") at The Southern Baptist Theological Seminary, March, 1976 (tape recording on file at Boyce Library).

[2]Samuel Miller, "The Care of Souls--And Faith" (Louisville: Boyce Library, The Southern Baptist Theological Seminary, 1963), p. 1. (Mimeographed.)

[3]Ibid., p. 3.

[4]Theodore F. Adams, "Preaching With Power and Purpose" (Louisville: Boyce Library, The Southern Baptist Theological Seminary, 1956), p. 13. (Mimeographed.)

[5]H. Grady Davis, "The Personal Word" (Louisville: Boyce Library, The Southern Baptist Theological Seminary, 1962), pp. 9-11. (Mimeographed.)

[6]Ibid., p. 9.

[7]Ibid., p. 10.

[8]Ibid.

[9]Ibid., p. 11.

[10]Davis, "The Individual and Community" (Louisville: Boyce Library, The Southern Baptist Theological Seminary, 1962), p. 35. (Mimeographed.)

[11]Ibid., p. 26.

[12]George Buttrick, "Preaching In This Present Age" (Louisville: Boyce Library, The Southern Baptist Theological Seminary, 1944), pp. 19-21. (Mimeographed.)

[13]Ibid., p. 19.

[14]Ibid., p. 20

[15]Ibid., p. 21.

[16]William Muehl, "A Sense of Loss" (Louisville: Boyce Library, The Southern Baptist Theological Seminary, 1975), p. 5. (Mimeographed.)

[17]Ibid.

[18]John Claypool, in a lecture ("From Preaching to Liturgies") at The Southern Baptist Theological Seminary, March, 1974. (Tape recording on file at Boyce Library).

[19]John Mackay, "God's Unveiled Secret" (Louisville: Boyce Library, The Southern Baptist Theological Seminary, 1948), p. 7. (Mimeographed.)

[20]Ibid.

[21]John Mackay, "The Gospel of God For The Nations" (Louisville: Boyce Library, The Southern Baptist Theological Seminary, 1948), p. 40. (Mimeographed.)

[22]Paul Scherer, "A Great Gulf Fixed" (Louisville: Boyce Library, The Southern Baptist Theological Seninary, 1957), p. 4. (Mimeographed.)

[23]Scherer, "The Word in Search of Words," p. 21.

[24]Ibid.

[25]Donald Macleod, in a lecture ("Theology Gives Meaning and Shape to Worship") at The Southern Baptist Theological Seminary, March, 1970. (Tape recording on file at Boyce Library).

[26]John Claypool, "From Preaching to Liturgies."

[27]Ibid.

[28]H. H. Farmer, "The Preacher and Persons," Review and Expositor, XLIII, No. 4 (1946), pp. 403-17.

[29]Ibid., p. 406

[30]Ibid.

[31]Ibid., pp. 406-7.

[32]Ibid., p. 407.

[33]Ibid., pp. 410-11.

[34]Ibid., p. 413.

CHAPTER V

SUMMARY AND EVALUATION

In this book I have studied the available lectures in the Mullins series in an effort to see how much material has been offered on the three aspects of communication which Aristotle deemed essential, namely, the speaker, speech, and audience. By the amount and quality of the materials found, I have concluded that the Mullins lecturers also have felt that Aristotle's triadic elements are of great importance. Especially is this true of the speaker and message.

Summary

Regarding the speaker, personality is seen as an important factor in determining effectiveness. The speaker, as a person, is to possess good self knowledge, and should be strong of character. He is not to be diffident, but should be tactful and deferential. He must love his hearers and must not merely excoriate them to meet his own needs. He becomes one with his message, for the power of the Gospel comes to and through him.

The speaker is to possess specific qualifications, including a sense of calling, a strong awareness of God, identification with his people, strong personal convictions, and moral purity.

He is to prepare himself for his task through education, attention to personal health, and by expanding his perceptive powers, especially through art. The speaker's attitudes influence his work. He is to have a catholic spirit, possess a professional attitude, and be existentially involved in his work.

The message has at its heart the Gospel.
Involved also are the Word of God, the element
of judgment, awareness of contemporary events
and thinking, and an inviting ingredient.

Sources of the message include revelation,
experience with Christ, the preacher's own
creativity, and the Bible. The style of the
message is important to its communicative quality. Most of the men who dealt with delivery
agreed that delivery of the message is best
done without notes, and in a natural, relaxed
manner.

The setting of the message is worship. The
form of the sermon is important in relation to
its content and its intention. Craftsmanship,
if poorly done, can debilitate the sermon. Thus,
great care is to be given craftsmanship.

The audience is important since it is from
that context, that is, from within the Christian
congregation, that the Word of God comes. The
contemporary congregation has a mentality shaped
by mass media. A speaker needs to take this
into account when trying to address an audience.
He needs to establish a strong rapport with his
hearers in order to communicate effectively with
them.

EVALUATION

In evaluating the Mullins lectures, I begin
with a more generalized critique and then move to
a more specific evaluation. First, general
impressions are given.

Some of the stronger lectures in terms of
clarity of thought, force of content, and style
include those by George Buttrick, H. H. Farmer,
Paul Scherer, Samuel Miller, Kelley Miller Smith,
and William Muehl. Some of the weaker ones,

using the same criteria as above, include the
lectures of Robert J. McCracken, Theodore
Adams, Horton Davies, and Roger Fredrikson.

Weaknesses

More specifically, obvious elements essential to preaching were only vaguely touched on
or ignored completely. These include the
following items: Little attention was given
to the preacher's sense of "call;" little was
said about the Bible; relatively little was
said about the audience; nothing was said about
women in the ministry; not much space was devoted to prayer as related to the sermon; the
aspect of rhetoric as related to preaching
found little consideration in these lectures.
Further, the whole matter of text, with three
minor exceptions, was untouched; the development of a theme was not expanded; the use of
illustrations found no positive treatment in
the lectures. The element of imagination as a
separate category in homiletics scarcely was
dealt with, nor was the matter of the use of
voice, gestures, or pacing dealt with adequately.

Categorization of the Lectures

The Lectures fall roughly into the following standard categories of homiletics.

1. The Philosophy of Preaching: Buttrick,
    Farmer, Muehl.

2. The Theology of Preaching: Luccock,
    Mackay, Manson, Scherer, Davis, Miller,
    Phillips, Sittler, Macleod, Claypool,
    McCord.

3. The Technique of Preaching: MacLennan,
    McCracken, Adams, Smith, Fredrikson.

4. The History of Preaching: Guinn, Davies.

In all, the theology and philosophy of
preaching were dealt with adequately. As shown
above, these two categories dominate. It seems
that the lecturers felt that students could get
help on history, rhetoric, and technique from
many sources. Thus, they tried to lay a firm
foundation as to the "why" of preaching.

Recommendations

Based on the Mullins lectures of past
years, the following recommendations may be
made regarding matters of topics, helpfulness
to the seminary, and persons to deliver the
lectures.

1. Have someone deal with women in
   ministry.

2. Have someone deal with the Bible in the
   sermon, possibly James Smart, David
   Buttrick, Ernest Best, or Leander Keck.

3. Have someone deal with creative preaching, possibly John Killinger.

4. Have some lecturer speak on the relationship between preaching and communication theory, possibly Merrill Abbey.

5. Have some scholar deal with inductive
   preaching, possibly Fred B. Craddock.

6. The seminary should always get a copy
   of the manuscript from each lecturer.
   Copies of these manuscripts should be
   made available to students.

BIBLIOGRAPHY

1. The E.Y. Mullins Lectures

Adams, Theodore F. "A Preacher Looks at His
    Preaching." Louisville: Boyce Library,
    The Southern Baptist Theological Seminary,
    1956. (Mimeographed.)

Allen, J. P. "What Kind of Gospel?" Sermon at
    The Southern Baptist Theological Seminary,
    Louisville, 1968. Tape available at Boyce
    Library.

_____. "The Next to Last Straw." Sermon
    at The Southern Baptist Theological Semi-
    nary, Louisville, 1968. Tape available
    at Boyce Library.

_____. "Life's Indefinable Categories."
    Sermon at The Southern Baptist Theological
    Seminary, Louisville, 1968. Tape available
    at Boyce Library.

_____. "Open Other Channels." Sermon at
    The Southern Baptist Theological Seminary,
    Louisville, 1968. Tape available at the
    Boyce Library.

Buttrick, George A. "What Is the Gospel?"
    Review and Expositor, XL, No. 2 (1943),
    151-166.

_____. "Power--and the Man," Review and
    Expositor, XL, No. 3 (1943), 279-295.

_____. "The Craftsmanship of Preaching."
    (A and B) Louisville: Boyce Library, The
    Southern Baptist Theological Seminary, 1943.
    (Mimeographed.)

_____. "Preaching in this Present Age."
    Louisville: Boyce Library, The Southern
    Baptist Theological Seminary, 1943.
    (Mimeographed.)

Claypool, John R. "Preaching and the Preacher." Lecture at The Southern Baptist Theological Seminary, Louisville, 1974. Tape available at Boyce Library Audio-Visual Center.

_____. "The Authority of the Preacher." Lecture at The Southern Baptist Theological Seminary, Louisville, 1974. Tape available at Boyce Library.

_____. "Listening and Preaching." Lecture at The Southern Baptist Theological Seminary, Louisville, 1974. Tape available at Boyce Library.

_____. "From Preaching to Liturgies." Lecture at The Southern Baptist Theological Seminary, Louisville, 1974. Tape available at Boyce Library.

Davies, Horton. Worship and Theology in England: From Newman to Martineau, 1850-1900. "Worship and Theology in England," Vol. 4. Princeton: Princeton University Press, 1962, 282-348.

Davis, Elam. "The God Who Creates From Nothing." Sermon at The Southern Baptist Theological Seminary, Louisville, 1967. Tape available at Boyce Library.

_____. "On Treating People as Persons." Sermon at The Southern Baptist Theological Seminary, Louisville, 1967. Tape available at Boyce Library.

_____. "The Church and the Social Dilemma." Sermon at The Southern Baptist Theological Seminary, Louisville, 1967. Tape available at Boyce Library.

_____. "God and Life." Sermon at The Southern Baptist Theological Seminary, Louisville, 1967. Tape available at Boyce Library.

Davis, H. Grady. "Reappraisals of Preaching."
Louisville: Boyce Library, The Southern
Baptist Theological Seminary, 1962.
(Mimeographed.)

Farmer, H. H. "Preaching and Worship," Review
and Expositor, XLIII, No. 3 (1946), pp.
243-260.

_____. "The Preacher and Persons," Review
and Expositor, XLIII, No. 4 (1946), 403-418.

_____. "The Preacher and Culture," Review
and Expositor, XLIV, No. 1 (1947), 34-49.

Finegan, Jack. "God, Jesus, and Life." Sermon
series at The Southern Baptist Theological
Seminary, Louisville, 1969. Tapes available at Boyce Library.

Fredrikson, Roger. "Renewal in the Church."
Lecture series at The Southern Baptist
Theological Seminary, Louisville, 1976.
Tapes available at Boyce Library.

Guinn, G. Earl. "That the Ministry Might Not Be
Ashamed." Lecture at The Southern Baptist
Theological Seminary, Louisville, 1960.
Tape available at Boyce Library.

Luccock, Halford E. "What Literature Can Do For
the Preacher," Review and Expositor, XLII,
No. 3 (1945), 255-265.

_____. "A Hunger For Affirmations," Review
and Expositor, XLII, No. 4 (1945), 392.

McCord, James I. "Theological Education and the
Preacher." Lecture series at The Southern
Baptist Theological Seminary, Louisville,
1977. Tapes available at Boyce Library.

McCracken, Robert J. The Making of the Sermon.
New York: Harper and Brothers, 1956.

Mackay, John A. "Our World and God's Gospel." Louisville: Boyce Library, The Southern Baptist Theological Seminary, 1948. (Mimeographed.)

MacLennan, David A. Pastoral Preaching. Philadelphia: The Westminster Press, 1955.

Macleod, Donald. "Crisis in Preaching." Lecture at The Southern Baptist Theological Seminary, Louisville, 1970. Tape available at Boyce Library.

_____. "The Identity of the Preacher." Lecture at The Southern Baptist Theological Seminary, Louisville, 1970. Tape available at Boyce Library.

_____. "Theology Gives Meaning and Shape to Worship," The Princeton Seminary Bulletin, LXVIII, No. 2 (1975), pp. 37-47.

_____. "What Are You Doing In the Church?" Higher Reaches. London: The Epworth Press, 1975, 73-81.

Manson, T.W. The Servant-Messiah: A Study of the Public Ministry of Jesus. Cambridge: Cambridge University Press, 1966; Grand Rapids: Baker Book House, 1977 reprint.

Miller, Samuel H. "The Minister's Workmanship." Louisville: Boyce Library, The Southern Baptist Theological Seminary, 1963. (Mimeographed.)

Muehl, William. "A Sense of Loss." Louisville: Boyce Library, The Southern Baptist Theological Seminary, 1975. (Mimeographed.)

_____. "The Height of Creativity." Louisville: Boyce Library, The Southern Baptist Theological Seminary, 1975. (Mimeographed.)

_____. "The Depth of Judgment." Louisville:
Boyce Library, The Southern Baptist Theological
Seminary, 1975. (Mimeographed.)

_____. "The Breadth of Compassion." Louis-
ville: Boyce Library, The Southern Baptist
Theological Seminary, 1975. (Mimeographed.)

Scherer, Paul. "The Word in Search of Words."
Louisville: Boyce Library, The Southern Baptist Theological Seminary, 1957. (Mimeographed.) (New York: Harper and Row, 1965.)

Sittler, Joseph. The Anguish of Preaching. Philadelphia: Fortress Press, 1967.

Smith, Kelley Miller. "Preaching and Social
Crises." Lecture series at The Southern Bap-
tist Theological Seminary, Louisville, 1971.
Tapes available at Boyce Library.

Steimle, Edmund. "Lover's Quarrel." Sermon at
The Southern Baptist Theological Seminary,
Louisville, 1972. Tape available at Boyce
Library.

_____. "The Waiting Game." Sermon at The
Southern Baptist Theological Seminary, Louisville, 1972. Tape available at Boyce Library.

_____. "Children and Angels." From Death to
Birth. Philadelphia: Fortress Press, 1973,
77-86.

2. Secondary Sources

Abbey, Merrill R. Communication in the Pulpit and
Parish. Philadelphia: The Westminster Press,
1973.

Baxter, B. B. The Heart of the Yale Lectures.
Grand Rapids: Baker Book House, 1971
reprint.

Berlo, David K. The Process of Communication.
    New York: Holt, Rinehart, and Winston,
    1960.

The Rhetoric of Aristotle, trans. by Lane
    Cooper. New York: D. Appleton & Co.,
    1932.

INDEX

103

ABOUT THE AUTHOR

Don M. Aycock is a native of Evangeline, Louisiana. He is a graduate of Louisiana College,
(B.A.), and Southern Baptist Theological Seminary,
(M. Div. and Th. M.). He has done further work
at Mansfield College, Oxford University.
Don has written articles for denominational
magazines and journals. In addition to articles,
he has co-written a book of prayers and devotions
for seminarians with his wife, Carla. It is
entitled, Not Quite Heaven (Lima, Ohio: C.S.S
Publishers)
A lover of the outdoors, Don enjoys hunting
and fishing, along with hiking.
At the present time he is the Pastor of the
West Side Baptist Church in Louisville, Kentucky.

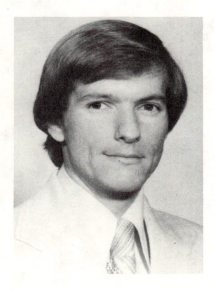

105